THE GREAT BLUE DREAM

THE GREAT BLUE DREAM

Inside the Mind of the Mountaineer

ROBERT LEONARD REID

HUTCHINSON
LONDON

This edition first published in 1992 by
Hutchinson

Random Century Group Ltd
20 Vauxhall Bridge Road, London SW1V 2SA

Random Century Australia (Pty) Ltd
20 Alfred Street, Milsons Point, Sydney, NSW 2061, Australia

Random Century New Zealand Ltd
18 Poland Road, Glenfield, Auckland, New Zealand

Random Century South Africa (Pty) Ltd
PO Box 337, Bergvlei, 2012, South Africa

A catalogue record for this book is available from the British Library

Printed and bound in Great Britain by
Biddles Ltd, Guildford and Kings Lynn

ISBN 0 09 175429 1

For Carol

Contents

Introduction

A century ago, British man of letters and mountain climber Leslie Stephen published *The Playground of Europe*, a collection of articles based on Stephen's more than two decades of climbing in the Alps of Switzerland and France. Erudite, witty, brimming with splendid descriptions of the mountains, the book quickly gained a wide readership. Today it is justly regarded as one of the great classics of mountaineering literature.

Stephen was one of those quaint gentleman-adventurers that Victorian England produced in such abundance, a tweedy ascetic equally at home in an overstuffed chair at his club in Park Lane and on a forced bivouac at the Eiger-Joch. A distinguished biographer, political philosopher, and editor, he is today best remembered for a rather less deliberate contribution to literature, his daughter Virginia Woolf. In the mountains he was, strictly speaking, an amateur who climbed with a guide. Yet Stephen was no effete tourist who needed a beefy Swiss to haul him up the peaks. He could hack steps in steep ice, inch calmly upward on exposed rock, and in the approved mountaineering fashion plod on uncomplainingly for hours.

Rereading parts of Stephen's book recently, I was struck by how little has changed. Today's mountaineer, of course, enjoys an enormous

technical advantage over the climber of a century ago. Modern mountaineers accustomed to space-age metals and fibers would feel naked
taking on the Rothhorn or the Matterhorn, as Stephen did, equipped
with wooden alpenstock and hemp rope.

But mountaineering has never been about equipment, it is about
mountains; and when Stephen turns his attention to the pleasures of
climbing he speaks to the climber of today and, I think, of any day. His
accounts of hard travel on the glaciers of the Oberland, of whittling the
Rothhorn down to size, of sunset on Mont Blanc are surprisingly up-
to-date. They bristle with passages that any climber will recognize and
thrill to. Throughout, he lays bare the myriad emotions that mountaineering inspires and every climber knows—love of danger, awe and
humility before the majesty and mystery of mountains, a sense of kin-
ship with nature.

In the end, however, Stephen cannot own up to these feelings, and
therein lies the glaring distinction between today's climber and the
climber of a century ago. The pathologically reserved Victorian male
was permitted a single emotion, an affection for the picturesque. The
intellect reigned supreme and from that high altar it demanded neat,
decisive, dispassionate answers to every question, even those which
were unanswerable. However complex Stephen's view of the mountains—and complex it is, as his early articles attest—ultimately he is
constrained to present it to his readers simply and unequivocally: "The
fact is that that which gives its inexpressible charm to mountaineering
is the incessant series of exquisite natural scenes, which are for the
most part enjoyed by the mountaineer alone." As for mountaineering
itself, it is a sport, he insists, "strictly a sport—as strictly as cricket, or
rowing, or knurr and spell—and I have no wish to place it on a different
footing. The game is won when a mountaintop is reached in spite of
difficulties; it is lost when one is forced to retreat."

Few mountaineers I know are quite so sure of themselves; certainly
I am not. Modern climbers have experienced an emancipation of perception and experience quite as revolutionary as the world-change in

equipment and technique which separates them from the climbers of Stephen's day. Many mountaineers now, even those who are engaged in other professions, regard climbing as a way of life. These men and women are not afraid to admit to the variety of physical and psycho-logical attractions that mountains hold for them, and the gamut of emotions these attractions inspire. Like everyone else, they live in a technological age, one that in many ways is as stifling and as narrow-minded as the age of Victoria. Contrary by nature, however, they re-ject the modern faith in ultimate answers. On soaring ridges, in the wilderness of rock and snow, they have learned that the mountain de-fies analysis.

All of which is an attempt to justify the vacillations, contradictions, ambiguities, and shocking caprices of the present collection, one which seeks to extract a measure of meaning from my experiences climbing mountains and wandering the mountain wildernesses of the United States over the past twenty-five years. I hope the reader who is curious about the allure of mountains or the pleasures of climbing them will feel well rewarded, for herein I explain these timeless mys-teries simply, unequivocally, and finally, at least a dozen different ways. With a good deal of pride, I present these essays as a veritable treasure trove of final judgments and last words, each as fleeting as mayflies. Unlike Leslie Stephen, I cannot summarize and I cannot provide an irrevocable answer, because the moment I think at last I un-derstand is the moment I round a corner and discover a landscape of unimagined richness, one that quickens my pulse anew and renders obsolete all previous understanding. Mountaineering is not at all like cricket, and mountains are not like tennis courts or horseshoe pits. Rather, they are like poems, altering their features and deepening in meaning with every visit. It is no more possible to give a simple answer to the question "Why do you go to the mountains?" than it is to explain *Leaves of Grass* in twenty-five words or less. Mountaineer and poet alike engage in bold adventures of the imagination. Both experience the world as an ever-changing interplay of shadow and light, of tran-

quillity and storm. Mountain and poem, the objects of their endeav-
ors, stand as lasting monuments to the futility of ultimate explication.

That I have unearthed a multitude of answers from my encounters
with mountains does not mean I have unearthed all the answers. In
these essays certain themes predominate: hope, the interconnectedness of all life, the generosity and geniality of creation, the fantastical
nature of the world. These are the souvenirs I bring back from my travels, for I cannot leave the mountain behind when I return to the lowlands. It is this inability to separate mountain climber from urban
dweller which convinces me that the Euroamerican's much-heralded
break with nature is more a myth than a reality. Our roots still reach
deeply into the earth beneath us, but in an illusory world that appears
increasingly human-made and human-controlled, this elemental
connection is easily forgotten. My goal in writing these pieces has been
to furnish a reminder, to point the way home.

"Let us stop here a little while longer! It is good to rest on the summit, and to dream amongst the clouds for a few short moments in one's life."

GUIDO REY, *Peaks and Precipices*

The Great
Blue Dream

The Mountain
of Love
and Death

To him who in the love of nature holds
Communion with her visible forms, she speaks
A various language.
WILLIAM CULLEN BRYANT, *"Thanatopsis"*

M ountain climbers speak easily and often eloquently of the beauties of the grand arenas where they practice their dangerous sport. A man with whom I have climbed occasionally, a taciturn soul of not notably refined sensibilities, once said to me matter-of-factly that his first glimpse of Mount McKinley high above the Alaskan tundra reminded him of an enchanted cloud. Where love is the issue, the climber speaks mountains.

Love, yes, but what of death, the other great theme that figures so prominently in the drama of mountaineering? Here the climber is strangely tight-lipped. This seeming indifference to so commanding a presence puzzles those who do not climb, and is sometimes taken as proof of the mountaineer's foolhardiness, or ignorance, or derangement. A kinder explanation allows climbers their sanity. Their deep and sustained communion with death has left them, I believe, not indifferent to that essential truth but, rather, respectfully speechless. The insights into the nature of death they have gained while practicing their perilous craft are so complex and so precious that out of fear and wonder they have taken them into their hearts to contemplate in silence. I climbed for twenty years, and while the possibility of dying was something I rarely discussed with my friends in the climbing community—and never with those outside—I secretly carried on an ardent relationship with death all the years that I climbed. The apprehension I felt so often while climbing was mingled with curiosity and even affection; my fear was blended with bliss. The countenance of death, which once had terrified me, grew ever more alluring the more I studied that not unsightly face. The longer I climbed, the more comfortable I became with the notion that I could die content in the mountains. Death in the city continued to strike me as a bad idea, but death in the mountains seemed fitting and natural. It is worth remembering that Melville's Billy Budd was fearless in the face of death because he stood nearer to what his creator called "unadulterate Nature" than did his citified counterparts. I don't claim to have achieved the Handsome Sailor's complete acceptance of death, but in the natural surroundings of the mountains I overcame at least the worst of my fears. I think that the same can be said of many mountaineers.

To nonclimbers' regret, we keep our insights to ourselves. When called upon to explain why we climb, we turn to our more expressive friend love for an answer. Why, it's the beauty of the mountains, we say. It's the adventure, the exhilaration, the challenge, the camaraderie, the quest for our limits. It's . . . the view from the top! We climb because climbing is a joy, we say; we climb because climbing takes us closer to God.

All of which is true, but none, save possibly the last, suggests the full truth, that more than love animates our affairs with the high peaks.

One summer past, weary at last of my own twenty-year affair, certain that I had no more to gain from its peculiar glow, and overwhelmed by a series of unhappy and apparently significant events in my life, I laid down my rope and my ice axe and retired from the sport of mountaineering. In the months since, I've had an opportunity to reflect at length on the issue of death in the mountains and to cast off some of the climber's customary reserve. Let me, then, take a crack at the ever-popular question I referred to a moment ago. Mountaineers climb because they love the mountains, yes; but they climb too because climbing prepares them boldly and tenaciously for death, then guides them faithfully to the edge of another world, a world I now recognize as the world of the dead, and there allows them to dance, mountain after mountain, year after year, as close to death as it is possible to dance; which is to say, within a single step. They go, *not to die*—that is very important—but far from the tumult of the valley below to linger in safe communion with death, to feel the exquisite tension that separates it from life, to glimpse its radiant smile and comprehend its peace. Climbing is a way of studying the ultimate unknown. In the curious playgrounds of their sport, mountaineers learn what primitive peoples know instinctively—that mountains are the abode of the dead, and that to travel into the high country is not simply to risk death but to risk understanding it.

Guido Rey, a Swiss who climbed at the turn of the century, wrote beautifully and compellingly of the joys of mountaineering. Seeking to explain why climbers court death in their quest for the summit, Rey made the following frequently quoted observation: "It is important to affirm and prove that we go to the mountains to live and not to die."

What he said is true, I think, but the way he said it is greatly misleading. By postulating a dichotomy between life and death that, through experience, the climber knows to be false, Rey inhibits a full understanding of the reasons people climb. It is precisely because life and death are not disparate conditions but, rather, gentle extensions of one another that the mountaineer moves so easily from one to the edge of the other. Rey meant to say that in the mountains we discover and express the beauty of life; what he failed to say but what is central to his meaning is that we cannot do so without glorying in the quiddity of death. Frequent confrontation with death is essential to mountaineering, not because, as Rey would have it, death can thereby be defied, but because it can thereby be tasted.

Who can admit to so mad an appetite! Countless times I have touched my tongue to the illicit brew, then, pulling back quickly, flopped onto a narrow ledge or trudged exhausted from a storm or felt the wicked angle of the snow beneath my feet lean back gently—and the joy that I knew each time surpassed words. Is it true that this joy at my return to life told only half the story . . . that there had been unspeakable joy, too, as I'd stood wide-eyed at the edge of the abyss, gazing silently and gratefully into the great darkness beyond?

Of all the sports that place responsibility for safety directly in the hands of the participants, mountaineering is by far the most dangerous. The death rates for parachuting and hang-gliding are slightly higher, but in both sports a failure of equipment rather than the victim's lack of experience or skill is most often the cause of death. Horse-racing, too, suffers a higher fatality rate, for not altogether different reasons. A safe outing at the downs depends on the successful performance not of a piece of technical equipment but of a highly tuned animal. Should the animal untune mid-race, the hapless jockey will be launched groundward as gaily and irrevocably as some wingless sky diver or hang-glider, perhaps with a dozen charging steeds waiting to trample him when he arrives.

Mountaineering equipment fails too, but rarely. What is unique to mountaineering is that so many things can go wrong. The climber who hopes to survive to old age must be prepared to overcome scores of potentially fatal hazards on every climb, and thousands in a typical career. That may sound daunting, but it is one of the sport's principal attractions. Mountain climbers positively relish the almost perfect rigor of their discipline's cardinal directive: Go to the edge and perform flawlessly, and you will survive (probably) to go to the edge again.

How delicious! Few choose this most exacting of pastimes because few can abide such punch-pulling reassurances. The best estimates put the number of serious recreational climbers in the United States at no more than thirty or forty thousand. (Bowling, the most popular sport, attracts a thousand times that number—some forty million devotees. No doubt the number would dwindle if each gutter ball were to prove fatal.) From the ball games of ancient Mexico to the gladiatorial contests of imperial Rome to the dangerous sports of today, none that I know of has formulated a system for choosing winners and losers that is quite as equitable as the system employed in mountaineering. Other sports that mete out death regularly do so arbitrarily or capriciously (recall our skydiver and jockey, now quite terminal aeronauts). Unlike these, mountaineering is exceedingly just, because it is self-refereeing. Penalties are assessed not by judges or umpires but by climbers themselves, who are left to bring disaster down upon their heads or not, as they choose.

The system is not foolproof: occasionally innocent climbers are done in by circumstances beyond their control. Usually, however, a flawless performance guarantees another sunrise, another brushing of the teeth and packing of the lunch, another trip to the edge. Historically this has held true regardless of the climber's race, color, creed, class, gender, or nationality, making mountaineering perhaps the most democratic of all sports.

How is this flawless performance achieved? Don't fall: that's central. By choosing routes that are within one's level of ability and preparing mentally and physically for the climb, one should be able to get to the top without falling. Don't freeze to death: easy—carry the right clothing and use it properly.

But the list is so long! Each threat can in theory be averted by the prudent climber—but after a long, exhausting, tension-filled day, with steep slopes ahead, the weather turning, and miles to go before camp is reached, will the climber in fact act prudently? A rappel is a doubled rope which one attaches to the mountainside to facilitate descent. One mountaineering humorist has identified two dozen ways in which a rappel can go wrong. Jim Madsen, an outstanding climber of a generation ago, zipped off the end of one on Yosemite's El Capitan and fell half a mile to his death. Marty Hoey was killed on Mount Everest when she failed to secure her waist harness properly and fell free of the rappel rope. The beautiful long red hair of a woman I know was sucked into a rappel braking device just as she started down the ropes on Wyoming's Grand Teton. She dangled in pain and horror a hundred feet above the ground for half an hour, but survived her ordeal by cutting off all her hair with a pocketknife.

A lovely day turns foul, a beautiful chunk of granite sails toward your unhelmeted head, a ten-thousand-year-old handhold that you failed to test snaps off at last . . . Climbers in Yosemite have completed brilliant multi-day ascents on walls several times the height of the Empire State Building, then been swept to their deaths as they crossed swollen streams during the easy jaunt home. Once on vertical rock in desert country I reached for a crack, inserted my fingers, stepped up, stared into the steely eyes of a rattlesnake coiled two feet from my hand. At such jolly times will one indeed perform flawlessly? I kept moving and the snake inexplicably allowed me to pass. Skilled but startled climbers have fallen to their deaths in just these circumstances.

The cumulative effect of this delirium of hazards is a fatality rate that one recent set of statistics shows to be seventeen times higher than that of mountaineering's nearest non-equipment-dependent competitor, college football, and forty times higher than that of boxing. Ten percent of those who attempt to climb mountains in the Himalaya die trying. Overall, one in two hundred climbers is killed in the practice of the sport.

One cannot climb for long without meeting someone who is marked. I have a friend who three times has lost a companion on a climb. Late one chill March afternoon, as the wind howled and a vanilla-colored sun slunk down behind a nameless peak in California's High Sierra, I watched in fascination as a ripple in the snow high on the east face of the mountain grew gently and beautifully into the wild rush of an avalanche. Starry-eyed at my side, safely out of the range of fire, stood a wonderful climber named Vera Watson. I didn't know her well and it wasn't an avalanche that eventually ended her life, but I have never forgotten the comment she made as we watched the snow pouring down that peak: "There will be lots bigger ones than that where I'm heading."

Where she was heading was Annapurna, the tenth highest mountain in the world. Six months later, as she climbed steep ice at 25,000 feet, Vera Watson was hit by falling ice or rock or otherwise knocked off balance—no one knows exactly how it happened. She fell twelve hundred feet to her death.

We are silent in the face of these tragedies. Three times I have attended meetings of mountaineering clubs where the deaths-in-action of members were announced. Each time the assembled solemnly inquired into the nature of the offending accident, then took up other business. When a death occurs on an expedition, the survivors bury their fallen comrade with suitable honors, then proceed with the climb. What explains this urge to continue? Is it callousness? Inertia? Numbness? Blindness? Or perhaps Santayana's fanaticism—a redoubling of effort when the aim has been forgotten. The Greek poets tell us of an island called Naxos and a princess named Ariadne who waited there patiently for her death. A ship arrived and with it the god Bacchus, who was destined to become Ariadne's lover and savior. Somehow she was blind to his identity and greeted him as the messenger of death. Can it be that the mountaineer, too, somehow confuses love and death, and in the midst of tragedy carries on as though passion can atone for or even overcome death?

I think of a climber I knew, a woman named Dina Lombard, who was drawn to the unspeakable beauty of a 14,000-foot mountain in northern California called Shasta, a mountain known to have supernatural powers. In winter, when it hovers white and radiant over the landscape, uncanny in its vastness and its tranquillity, Shasta is a transcendentally beautiful mountain—and a brutal and unforgiving one. Not far from the summit, late one February afternoon, Dina and a companion were engulfed by a storm of unimaginable ferocity. Taking pathetic shelter among a few scattered boulders, the two anchored themselves firmly to the steep slope and prepared to wait out the storm. During the night their food blew away and their feet froze. In the morning, after three failed attempts, they managed to descend a short distance through the still raging storm. On the edge of a crevasse they fashioned a small snow cave. Dina crawled in and her companion closed the entrance with her pack, then set out in the hope of securing food and a stove at a lower camp. The following day, during a lull in the storm, he reascended to the shelter. Where the cave had been, now only one thing remained: the pack and the snow had been blown away, and Dina lay dead on the lip of the crevasse.

Those who had known her might well have decided never to climb Shasta, or at least never to climb it in winter. For me, perhaps, like Ariadne, confused between love and death, the effect of this tragedy was precisely the opposite. My love for Shasta was deepened; so enraptured, I needed to know her better. I believed that in Shasta's winds I would feel something of the peace of Dina Lombard, in its swirling mists catch a glimpse of the place where she had gone. So it was that in a later winter I made the arduous ascent of the mountain. On an afternoon of such splendor and clarity that I seemed to be moving through timeless space, I came at last onto Shasta's icebound summit and saw the sky go black and the earth fall away at my feet. The cold air bristled with the scent of galaxies and nebulae. To the north, where mountains had once stood now silver moons hung beaming in the dying sun. It came to me that I had climbed to the center of the universe. I stood for a moment, taking it in, and then I began to weep. My tears were born of ecstasy and heartbreak alike—tears for the beauty of the world, tears for the gentleness of death.

A book called *The Conquest of Everest* by Sir John Hunt brought me to the high country. Growing up in Pennsylvania, where mountain climbers were about as common as crocodiles, I knew nothing of the sport until at sixteen, more or less at random I selected Hunt's account of the first ascent of the world's tallest peak for an English-class book report. In those days it was my habit to hang out in the public library—not for the reading matter, mind you, but for several studious and quite charming girls who also hung out there, and to whom I aspired greatly. When my own charm failed, as it often did, I sometimes wandered the stacks in search of strength and courage, and occasionally I located a book instead.

On the evening before my report was due I pulled the Hunt from a shelf and took it to a long oak table where a rabble of whispering teenagers, including two of my inamoratas, were seated. Perhaps I fancied that Janie or Susie would be impressed by my choice. Rather gravely, I expect, after checking to see that both were watching, I opened the book and began to survey its contents.

I was astonished and delighted to discover that, quite by accident, I had made a brilliant choice. Among the many chapters of the book was one entitled "The Summit," written not by principal author John Hunt but by Edmund Hillary, the man who with Tenzing Norgay had been the first to set foot on the top of the world. Clearly Hillary's contribution was the climax of the story. I saw that I could base my report on his very brief memoir (it was only sixteen pages long) and disregard the rest of the book altogether. If I hurried I could finish in time for a cherry Coke with Susie. (I discovered the pleasures of reading entire books only later in life and have since read all of the *Conquest*. I can attest now, on belatedly complete evidence, that Hunt's part is rather plodding and colorless—I believe I mentioned that in my original report—but that Hillary's is, indeed, worth a read. My mountaineering instincts, it seems, were solid from the beginning.)

My first brush with the high peaks, then, I can now recreate for you with some accuracy. It is a lusty spring evening in 1959 in Titusville, Pennsylvania, altitude 220 feet. Inside the Benson Memorial Library, a probably climbable structure of, as I recall, somewhat craggy construction, the scent of pretty girl hangs like edelweiss in the air, the whispering and flirting have reached Himalayan proportions, and Mrs. Doris Krimble, a librarian icy of demeanor and glacial of stare, has just issued her final warning for the hundredth time. Momentarily abashed, I turn to page 197 of the book and begin to read:

> Early on the morning of May 27th I awoke from an uneasy sleep feeling very cold and miserable. We were on the South Col of Everest. My companions in our Pyramid tent, Lowe, Gregory, and Tenzing, were all tossing and turning in unsuccessful efforts to gain relief from the bitter cold. The relentless wind was blowing in all its fury and the constant loud drumming on the tent made deep sleep impossible. Reluctantly removing my hand from my sleeping bag, I looked at my watch. It was 4 A.M. In the flickering light of a match, the thermometer lying against the tent wall read −25° Centigrade.

Neither the library's craggy construction nor Mrs. Krimble's glacial stare could have prepared me for the shock: it was staggering. The events and conditions that Hillary described were as Balinese to me. Yet something in his words struck a primal nerve in me. I emerged from my reading on fire. One sentence stood out, one that I now know touches on two of mountaineering's most persistent and addicting pleasures: "Our faculties seemed numbed," wrote Hillary of the summit pair's condition during the descent, "and time passed as if in a dream."

Something of that numbing and that dreaminess came over me. Suddenly I longed to be in some faraway place, alone in elemental conditions, surrounded by ice and space and silence. I remember seeing myself wandering through such a place, moving in a thick ether, experiencing an all-consuming peace. Mountains, which I had never seen or even thought about before, were suddenly mysterious, thrilling places—enchanted clouds. Perhaps they embodied the remembered joys of my childhood, or my fantasies of life on another world. Historian Roderick Nash, who has traced the human attitude toward wilderness over several thousand years, has concluded, quite correctly, I think, that wilderness has never existed. Wilderness, says Nash, is a feeling about a place, part of what he calls "the geography of the mind." The geography of my mind, sketched in the distant past and fleshed out in 1959, is a high and snowy place, shrouded in mist and haunted by an ethereal quiet. There are trees and rocks about, and even, somehow, bright flowers and narrow winding streams. High above float mountaintops, their shadowy ramparts just visible where the mist is wearing thin. They seem light years distant, yet so near that I hold my breath at the sight. Standing in that landscape, as I often have since that visionary evening so long ago, I glimpse what poet Eunice Tietjens has called "the white windy presence of eternity."

It is hours before dawn. In a blackness complete but for a creamy ellipse of mountainside awakened by my headlamp, I zigzag up the glacier. Two steps and rest, two steps and rest, two steps and rest. In my solitude I focus on the soft report that rises from my boots: lub dub, lub dub, lub dub. *I stop to catch my breath, drive in my axe, fall on it like a drunkard at the bar. Alchemy accomplished. The genial ellipse, now inches from my eyes, transfigures into art: in each of a thousand snow crystals a perfect rainbow appears. I turn in excitement and then spot them, far away on the glacier below—seven twinkling lights, seven burning fires, seven kindred souls moving upward with me, warm Pleiades in the deep and distant sky.*

The storm is lifting at Bugaboo Col. Huddled beneath a slab of rock, my friend and I speak of two we know who have ascended into the storm. Hopeful at the turn in the weather, we venture onto the bleak snowscape to survey the prospect to the west.

Minutes pass. A wisp of cloud drifts past us through the col. A grand hush settles over the amphitheater.

Suddenly we are shouting and waving our arms. The two have made their decision: languidly, like dolphins at play, they descend through the mist, descend from the tower of death.

Mountains are a passive mystery, Annie Dillard has written. An eternal one, she might have added, for from the beginning of time mystics have found in mountains an unending source of wonder and inspiration. The indelible mark of the mystic is impatience at the necessity of waiting until death to unite with God. The restless one aspires to transcend the limitations of human experience, to overcome life, in order to achieve the dreamed-of unification on earth. Terrestrial unification is an exquisite resolution to the unbearable tension over the knowledge of death that stalks us all our days. An ex-climber reading about the techniques mystics use to accomplish their goal is struck by how closely they resemble mountaineers' own techniques. Mystic and mountaineer alike move heavenward through the practice of the ascetic arts: austerity, endurance, denial. The Dominican Henry Suso submitted to extremes of self-torture, bearing on his back a heavy cross studded with nails until God "did gladden the heart of the sufferer in return for all his sufferings." Jesus endured forty days in the wilderness, Buddha five years of self-denial, the Jainist Mahavira thirteen years of hunger, cold, pain, and sexual deprivation, bearing it all in silence.

I don't wish to suggest that a modern mountaineer's few days or weeks of hardship in any way compare with Buddha's five years or Mahavira's thirteen; yet raptures are reported by climbers often enough to suggest that thirteen years of deprivation may not be necessary to achieve the mystic consciousness. Cold, hungry, tired, celibate (the absence of sex in the mountains is one of the most interesting and least-discussed phenomena in mountaineering; young, vigorous climbers go cold turkey for weeks at a time in pursuit of their ends), the mountaineer toils upward hour after hour, day after day, bending low beneath an oppressive pack, bearing it all in silence. Mystic and mountaineer both practice extreme mind control (renowned rock climber Yvon Chouinard's directions for mastering difficult rock ring with the simplicity and directness of Zen: "Relax your mind, relax your mind, you've got to relax your mind"). Often a trance—Hillary's dream-state—is induced. Time may unfold at a wholly unnatural rate; a fall or a near-death experience that consumes only a fraction of a second may be perceived by the climber as an elaborate drama, with the harrowing events of each microsecond developed into a friendly, even captivating scene.

Sometimes a rarely seen part of the self is revealed. Usually this manifests itself as an overwhelming sense that another, usually unseen person is nearby. I experienced such a feeling once after spending several days alone in the wild northern reaches of Yosemite National Park. For some minutes I tried to find the "real" person I knew to be shadowing me. My invisible companion was, of course, myself, but it required unusual loneliness and isolation to allow me to see my hidden side—to know, as Eliot said, that there is always another walking beside me.

And then at last the payoff: Nirvana or the summit, depending upon your persuasion. A close reading of the critical texts suggests that the two may be identical. No sport that I know of has spawned a literature as introspective, as probing, or ultimately as religious as mountaineering. The sport causes climbers to experience unimaginable hardships and then, at the ends of their ropes, to plumb their souls for meaning. They emerge from their excursions to the edge of unknowing with insights into their spiritual natures that transcend the possibilities of mere sport. The literature is replete with tales of magic and mystery, of wild humor and terrible sadness and loss and then rebirth—all integral to the practice of climbing, all the result of protracted contact with the unseeable. A marvelous example of this class of writing is Hermann Buhl's stirring account of his 1953 solo ascent of Nanga Parbat, a 26,600-foot mountain in the Himalaya of Kashmir. In only nine pages Buhl manages to transport the reader from the depths of torment and despair to the heights of fantasy and ecstasy and, finally, to the triumph of the human spirit. As dawn breaks over the mountain we see Buhl moving steadily upward, "an undulating sea of summits" on all sides, a fine mist in the valley below. Alone and determined, he ascends past 24,000 feet, climbing hard snow and "bare, bluish iridescent ice. . . . How often had I dreamed of this moment!" he exults.

At 25,000 feet he begins to slow. Because he carries no oxygen, his body seems paralyzed, his lungs unable to expand properly. He fears he has reached the limit of his endurance.

Yet he goes on, moving slowly across Nanga Parbat's great Silver Plateau. There is no wind. The air is fearfully dry. A scorching sun beats down on him with Saharan fire and malice. The weight of his rucksack grows intolerable. He has no choice: after stuffing a few essential items into his pockets, he abandons his pack.

Willpower alone now carries him upward. He gives no thought to the movement of his legs. He is lost in a vivid dream of home. Making the first ascent of perhaps the world's most treacherous mountain (Nanga Parbat had already claimed thirty-one lives), he believes he is climbing a friendly peak in his native Tyrol.

Late in the day he surpasses 26,000 feet. Ahead rises a steep mass of boulders, the most technically difficult section of the climb. He surmounts these somehow, then, with one final effort, drops onto all fours and drags himself to the top.

"I was not, I must confess, at the time fully conscious of the significance of that moment, nor did I have any feeling of elation at my victory. I simply felt relieved to be on top and to know that all the sweat and toil of the ascent were behind me."

As Buhl stands atop the peak, the highest creature on earth, he watches bemusedly as the sun sinks below the horizon in the west. Suddenly the air is bitterly cold. Unable to think clearly, he makes a terrible mistake: he leaves his ice axe on the summit. Now the problems compound. As he descends a steep ice slope in the murky dusk, a crampon drops from his foot. He is left "like a stork standing on the smooth hard surface." Buhl continues the harrowing descent with the aid of one crampon and a pair of ski poles.

Darkness finds him marooned on a fifty-degree slope a few hundred feet below the summit. All his bivouac equipment lies far below, in his abandoned rucksack. He crawls onto a rock, then pulls on a thin sweater, his only emergency clothing. Through the long night he stands atop the rock, dancing to keep his feet from freezing.

At dawn his feet are numb, his boots glazed with ice. With surpassing care he moves down perilous slopes, unaware of the passage of time. He is not alone: throughout the day another descends with him. The two become a team. When Buhl misplaces a pair of gloves, it is his phantom companion who tells him they are lost.

The sun is again a torment. The descending climber is plagued by hunger and thirst. His mouth bleeds. He hears voices but no one comes to save him. He finds his pack and falls onto it, only to discover that he is unable to swallow the dry food. He takes a small drink, then sees two distant figures approaching.

"Oh, the joy of it. Someone was coming! I heard voices too, calling my name."

He watches the two specks below but they come no closer. At last he understands the bitter truth: his saviors are rocks on the mountainside.

Each step now requires a dozen breaths. He moves twenty or thirty yards, then collapses. His ordeal seems interminable. The sun is nearing the horizon. Buhl must reach safety soon, for he cannot survive another night in the open.

And then it is over. He staggers into the arms of a friend who has come to meet him. "He looked aged by twenty years," writes another. "His face, desiccated and deeply lined, bore the imprint of intolerable suffering." Buhl manages to mutter eight words, a simple report of his visit to the edge: "Yesterday was the finest day of my life."

Every climber recognizes those words. Few have suffered as Buhl did, but many have experienced a day in the mountains as sublime and unforgettable as the one he so movingly recalled. Such emotion springs from a deep self-knowledge that I believe touches on the reality of love and death. That yearning lifts the climber again and again into the fabulous land of white gothic spires.

None of this could I have guessed in 1959. But something in Hillary's words touched me, and not long after, on a slip of paper I kept that bore the heading "Life List," I added two words: *Climb mountains*.

Seven years passed before I took my first step toward fulfilling that goal. Then, in the dead of winter in 1966, on an impulse available only to the young and the foolish, I agreed to join two friends on a four-day snowshoe traverse of the Franconia Ridge in the East's most arctic of ranges, the White Mountains of New Hampshire.

Of that hideous misadventure two remembrances stand out: the brain-curdling cold and the terror. My equipment was ludicrous. I slept in a Sears dacron sleeping bag designed, I believe, for summer in Mississippi. My pack was a Boy Scout knapsack barely large enough to carry my basic equipment, let alone an extra sweater or two; the over-flow I tied onto the outside of the pack with mailing twine. As I stumbled upward through the trees on the first day, nimble-fingered pine and hemlock branches untied my granny knots and sent an avalanche of cooking pots and canteens clanging down the mountainside.

The second night we camped in a blizzard in the saddle between Mount Lafayette and Mount Lincoln. As the wind screamed and the tent shook so violently I feared it and its precious contents would be hurled to the bottom of the mountain, I came to understand one thing—that I was surely going to die.

Now to understand that one is going to die is a useful and profound understanding, not often reached at such an early age. Of course, like

Saint Paul, I thought the end was near and designed my prayers accordingly. That death lay some years in the future was information denied to both Saint Paul and me, and thus in no way diminished the impact of our perceptions or altered our subsequent behavior. When I did not die on the spot, when I escaped unscathed from that wretched place, I vowed solemnly to return to the mountains as quickly as possible.

Two summers later I went west with my friends Leon and Henry Bills, and there in the Tetons of Wyoming I saw my first high mountains. I knew that I had to climb them. I had no idea how I would accomplish that seemingly impossible task, but, camped at their base, gazing up each day at faraway summits drifting in and out of clouds, I somehow guessed at the intimacy that is available only to the mountaineer, and longed to share in it. I was spellbound by one peak in particular. Teewinot was a perfect snow-draped triangle that swept up and up, ever narrower and more thrilling, to a wondrous pinnacle piercing the sky. By day she quickened my pulse; by night she haunted my dreams. She lay so close to my campsite that I began to know her habits and moods. As though courting her, I wove a sinuous dance at the mountain's foot—exploring her circling paths, dipping at midday into her refreshing streams, pausing in her cool shadows, withdrawing to admire her from afar.

One fine day my friends and I rented ice axes, purchased a length of goldline rope, and set off to consummate the mad affair. We were quite impetuous all the way, I think. It was our first time; we were hale and determined, but lacked style. Several times in my eagerness I dislodged large, efficient-looking rocks that sailed harmlessly past my companions (but woe to anyone below!). On steep snow I came loose but was saved by the rope, a stroke of luck that cheered us greatly. It became clear that we were not to be thwarted, so excellent was our mission.

As we approached the top I saw to my horror that the summit was a smooth rock the size and shape of a very large almond. On all sides the drop-off was terrible. It was evident that the final act would be a des-

perate business. The three of us looked at each other with blank faces.
I took a deep breath, said a heart-felt prayer, dropped to my hands and
knees, and crawled to the summit like a turtle.

From far below came a thin sound of cheering that failed to encour-
age me. I lay there hugging that inadequate slab of masonry as though
it were my dear mama. To distract myself I thought of other places I had
visited, nice places, low places.

Slowly then, after what seemed like an interminable length of time,
I began to gain confidence. Following careful and exhaustive planning, I rolled onto my back. Then I sat up and looked around.

My first impression was one of a curious drifting of time and space.
I seemed to be moving. I know now that I was. I liked it. Summits, I
quickly realized, are not the solid, precisely defined spots that are
shown on maps. Rather, they are capricious, meandering places,
whose locations, like those of electrons and small children, are incapable of being pinpointed at any given moment.

My senses came to attention. Below I saw my friends snapping pictures. I felt the wind and the dazzle of the nearby sun. I felt the top of
my head rubbing the sky. (I am now bald there; many climbers suffer
this affliction.) I gazed across a choppy ocean of space at the mountain
called the Grand Teton, a resplendent peak that reached even higher
into the heavens than the point where I hovered. Suddenly, for the first
time, I felt the terrible addiction of the mountaineer: *I wanted that one!*
I wanted, more precisely, the east ridge of the Grand Teton, a steep,
narrow, utterly bewitching buttress that sliced upward in one magnificent mile-long line from the glacier thousands of feet below me to the
very summit of the peak. That long and elegant route introduced me to
the aesthetic element of mountaineering: the east ridge of the Grand
Teton (or the Grand, as we soon began calling it) was desirable not simply because it led to the top of the peak, but because it was so beautiful.
From my lofty perch I studied it raptly: its explosive eruption in the glacier below, its urgent coalescence into great towers and gleaming black
ice and rock tumbled on snow, its dark aprons and white cornices and

inexorable upward thrust, now narrowing, now rushing, now only rock, now only snow, now only sky—

My eyes ran swiftly over the ridge, taking in more and more detail with each pass. I grew more familiar with my newfound beauty by the minute, more needful, and all I could think was . . . *to be there! to be there!*

It was beyond my present powers. But I vowed that one day, when I had perfected my skills, I would return to climb the ridge.

On the way down I fell. Descending a long and steep snowfield unroped, I slipped, dropped my ice axe (which I had no idea how to use anyway), and slid out of control for several hundred feet before crashing at an exciting rate of speed into a jumble of boulders at the bottom of the snow. I stood up, dusted myself off, waved triumphantly to my friends above, and continued the descent.

That was not our only near-miss. A few days later, as we approached the summit of Mount Moran, we were caught by a storm that leapt over the top of the peak at us. The morning had been beautiful; now freezing rain was pouring down and a wicked wind was whipping at our parkas. We were inexperienced but not stupid. We saw that our position on a tiny island of rock in the middle of a steep snow tongue was perilous. Quickly we crossed the snow to a more protected spot. A moment later a brilliant flash of light burst around us, followed almost instantly by an earsplitting clap of thunder. Fifty yards away a bolt of lightning reached out of the mist and blasted our recently departed island of rock to smithereens.

Nor was that all. After descending a pinnacle called Cube Point on rappel, I disengaged on what turned out to be very steep ground. Afraid to move, I simply stood stolidly at the base of the rappel. A few moments later my partner came flying down the ropes quite magnificently and crashed into me like a sandbag from the rafters. Together we rolled merrily down the slope until we came to rest in a lovely meadow filled with wildflowers.

Perhaps it was madness. And yet those early days held a hunger for the full length and breadth of experience and a thirst for the limits of emotion that were preeminently human and therefore preeminently sane. They helped me define what it meant to climb mountains. Utterly naive, burning with desire and fear, I set off each day to quell my foolish passion, and sometimes I succeeded. It was adventure of the grandest sort, adventure that ranked with the seat-of-the-pants voyages of Vasco da Gama and the wonderful, preposterous search for the Nile. The nation was about to land a man on the moon, and I couldn't have cared less. I began to see how easy it is to confuse adventure with flash, and to suppose that astronauts supported by worldwide communications networks and millionaires in zircon-coated balloons are adventurers. They are not. An adventure is a voyage into the unfamiliar. If you know what you're doing, it isn't an adventure. An adventure is a baring of your soul, not your wallet, an agreement to trust your wits rather than your digital homing device. Gentle reader, here is how to have an adventure: breathe deeply, throw down your defenses, *and take a flyer!*

In the years to come I took many. I became a typical mountaineer—modest ability, limited achievement, an amateur all the way but *possessed* by the mountains. That is to say, the backbone of the sport. I climbed year round, several days a month and usually several weeks during the summer. I began collecting books on mountaineering, and stamps and posters that depicted the peaks that had come to mean so much. Nearly every day for twenty years I studied maps and guidebooks, planned journeys to the far reaches of the universe. I climbed, or attempted to climb, some two hundred peaks throughout the United States and Canada; and on neighborhood crags—the Pinnacles, Wallface, Crow Hill, Goat Rock—I ascended hundreds of routes that only a rock climber could love: Twinkle Toes Traverse, Dick's Prick, Highway to Heaven, Portent. In the accustomed manner I had my brushes with death: a long fall in New York's Shawangunks that ended when the rope came tight around my waist; a slip unroped on a steep, exposed slab high on California's Mount Robinson. There I instinctively threw up an arm as I spun off; miraculously my hand flew into a crack above my head and jammed there, stopping me cold. The conviction grew that I was dancing ever closer to the edge. I dreamed of the east ridge of the Grand. Five times I climbed in the Tetons, ascending dozens of routes but never the ridge; it always felt beyond me. Several times I quit the sport, but I was always back within months.

Late one winter I returned to Pennsylvania from my home in California to be with my mother for the last time. She was eighty-one, and for more than a decade had suffered terribly as a series of increasingly debilitating illnesses had robbed her of her faculties one by one—her ability to walk, to feed herself, to turn over in bed, to see. Despite all of these hardships, she remained decidedly alive, something regarded as a miracle by most who knew her, and an added hardship as well. Even more amazing, she retained the capacity to settle into her wheelchair each morning with a measure of excitement about the day to come that was unfathomable.

In her final years her voice, never robust, left her almost entirely. Because my father was hearing-impaired, this led to frequent episodes of high comedy, to say nothing of maddening frustration, as she tried to make her needs known to him. During the day she did usually succeed, relying as much as anything on a kind of mental telepathy perfected over more than fifty years of marriage.

At night, however, something else was needed. My father, a sleeper of legendary soundness, tuned out the moment his head hit the pillow. To rouse him if she needed to get up in the middle of the night, my mother, who slept in a separate bed, required something more vigorous than mental telepathy.

So it was that during their final years together, my parents began joining their wrists with a length of cord each night when they retired. By giving a slight tug at her end—about all she was capable of—my mother was able to wake her partner at the other end of the cord.

Naturally, I saw this lifeline not only as a symbol of my parents' commitment to each other through half a century of marriage, but as an echo of the rope that connects two climbers as they work their way slowly and surely toward the summit of their mountain. The mountaineering technique is perfectly equitable, favoring neither climber; each protects the other during the ascent. The same was true of my parents, though I failed to recognize this fact at the time. Clearly my mother needed and received the protection of my father; what I didn't see was that my father, healthy and vital at his end of the lifeline, was equally dependent on the frail creature at the opposite end of the rope.

At last the difficulties of caring for his wife at home became too great, and my father was forced to find a place for her in a local nursing home. She moved into a sunny room with a sloe-eyed woman who sat rigidly upright in her bed, silent except for the blood-curdling moan she emitted every hour or so. Even now my parents remained intimately connected. With time out only to bolt down meals and hurriedly run errands, my father spent his days and evenings with my mother for more than a year. Seated beside her bed, he would tell her the latest news of my brother or me, or the torn-up sidewalk on Chestnut Street, or the dripping faucet in the kitchen. Often he read to her from the *Reader's Digest*. As the hours lengthened he would grow silent, sometimes falling asleep in his chair or gazing vaguely out the window at a small bed of flowers that was planted there as a reminder.

When I visited my mother last, she lay motionless in her bed, navigating some wonderful dream and preparing easily for what lay ahead. It was clear to me that, despite appearances, she understood everything I said. It was time for me to speak mountains. What I wanted most was to tell her it was all right for her to die, but the words would not come out. Like climbers, we had never much discussed death. Have I told you, she would whisper, pulling me close, that I want you to have Grandma's love seat? But that was circling the issue. And when the time came for me to sever the line that connected us, to ease the strain at her end through an act of selflessness and generosity, I could not do it. She lingered a month longer, and when I saw her next and kissed her cheek for the last time, it was cold as ice.

My father felt the loss of his companion of fifty-five years as a terrible blow. He seemed healthy, but during the next few months, each time we talked he told me that he would be joining her soon. I continued to fight: that's God's decision, I told him, not yours; you've got to take care of yourself, to do your best to go on. Reluctantly, he would agree, but with each call he sounded wearier, more despondent, and ever more certain of a fate he seemed to have taken firmly into his own hands.

I worried about him endlessly. With equal fervor I began to rejoice more and more in the wonder of life. I had recently emerged from the nightmare of divorce after losing to apparently greener pastures a wife of a dozen years. As that bad dream had progressed it had grown darker by the day. With little to show after ten years of struggle, I had given up hope of being a writer. My spirits, my self-esteem, and, not incidentally, my savings had dwindled to zero. I had lost a dear friend in a car accident and a beloved cat to old age. My closest friend had developed cancer. One morning he called me. "Bobby," he began in a faltering voice, and then he blurted it out: "I just tried to kill myself." So dreadful was that year that my friend's bungled suicide attempt emerged as one of the real high points.

And yet . . .

And yet I had survived. Bleeding and gasping, I had flopped onto a very narrow ledge, rolled over, checked my pulse, and found it to be ticking along as merrily as ever. Inexplicably, spring had blossomed once again in my life. I had met and fallen crazily in love with the woman whom music, the mountains, the moon, and the stars were created to celebrate. What's more, I had married her. I had left the job I'd taken during my earlier disillusionment and was recommitted to my writing. And to provide a fresh and exciting context for our astonishing new lives together, Carol and I had moved from suddenly tired California to young and hopeful New Mexico. Such was the spring when I began again, battered and patched but still warm at forty-three.

Came summer, the time to grapple with the mountains of my December dreams. I joined three friends, Kai Wiedman, Art Calkins, and John Flinn, for another go at the Tetons. When we arrived at our trailhead the knot in my stomach was tighter than it had ever been before. Never had I pulled on a pack and headed up a trail toward the high peaks with greater misgivings about my purpose than I did now. Beguiling mountains rose before me, beckoning as they always had, but I no longer craved union through the sacrament of climbing. My soul and my heart were not here, where they had to be if climbing was to have meaning; they were with my father in his grief; they were with Carol at home, where I longed to be, reveling in the beauties of life with her. As I headed into the high country I understood as I never had before how utterly stupid and unforgivable it would be for me to perish in the mountains.

On Mount Owen we climbed steep hard snow unroped, and in a gathering storm a few hundred feet from the summit traversed high over kingdom come. In a clouded vision I saw a body sailing silently into the void, saw three friends turning to watch the plunge. My boot skipped from a shallow footstep. I grabbed frantically at the snow, for a suspended moment felt the consummate peace of falling, the taking up into the blue, the serene absorption into interstellar matter . . .

I stopped, paralyzed with fear. Kai and Art went on; John huddled with me in the lee of a wall of rocks to await their return. As the wind sharpened and the first drops of rain slashed down on us, we foretold in hushed tones the epic that was unfolding: the cold and the wet, the awful wind, the icy ropes, the slick rock and scary rappels, the downclimbing in the dark, the miles and miles, the bivouac in the freezing rain. I faced it all with stark detachment. Already I was off the mountain; already I was in the place where I belonged.

Our friends arrived at the summit in a beehive of electricity. Kai's hardware buzzed at his waist as he touched the mountain's high point, a touch he knew might register as a microsecond of pleasure before dissolving in a white blindness of heat and light. On the way down Art slipped on steep snow but quickly arrested himself with his axe. I did not expect my friends to return but they did, quite suddenly. "We knocked the bastard off," announced Kai, echoing Hillary's words. Quickly we strung a rappel and slid off for home.

In sight throughout the descent, slanting up through the deepening light of slowly falling day, was the route I now knew I would never climb, the east ridge of the Grand Teton. I was too tired to appreciate my tragedy fully. From time to time I glanced up at the ridge, taking it in not as a beautiful woman I had lost but as a welter of problems I was relieved to have escaped. Deep in my heart stirred that irreconcilable sadness of never-to-be-realized dreams—but I would grieve tomorrow, not today.

The storm passed. We made a swift and safe descent to the base of the mountain, confident that we would be in camp by dark. Our route home led us across the Teton Glacier toward a yellow tent pitched in the towering beauty of ridge's shadow. We stopped to talk to the tent's inhabitants, two gentle and good-natured men named David Ryan and Paul Kopczynski. They told us in the understated yet burning tones I knew so well that at dawn they would go for the ridge.

I remember little of the conversation. I remember most my envy— envy at their youth and fitness, their quiet confidence and soaring ambition. The east ridge of the Grand! They were strong and prepared; I was old and tired and afraid. We talked disconnectedly, in that undertone of muted excitement and mutual respect I had used and heard so often with fellow climbers on the eve of an ascent. Little is said, but much of a mighty tradition of comradeship, vision, and passion is shared.

I needed just thirty-six hours more to make my decision. The next day we circled to the far side of the Grand. The following morning at daybreak we made for the summit of the mountain by a route that lay well within my capabilities, but no longer suited my purposes. A warm wind laden with the mist of dawn followed us upward to a rockbound alcove where the difficulties of the route began. There, as we paused momentarily for rest, the truth overcame me at last, and I knew that the time had come for me to pack it in. Whatever had brought me to this distant planet so often in the past had lost its hold on my heart. I had learned what the sport had to teach, and now I could take that knowledge and cherish it and grow with it for the remainder of my days. It was a gift for which I was profoundly grateful.

And one I would never share with David Ryan. David was thirty, the husband of Kathleen Ryan, a man from Cody, Wyoming, who made his living as a geologist. Rich with love for the high and the wild and the beautiful, he kayaked swiftly running rivers and climbed soaring snowy peaks. In the end, like many, he danced too close to the edge. Two nights before, I had wished him well as I turned to begin the final trudge back to my camp. Now, a few hundred yards from where I stood, he lay dead after a seven-hundred-foot fall from the east ridge of the Grand. He was one of the innocent, done in by circumstances beyond his control. Crossing a gully, he had been struck by a fusillade of rocks and carried helplessly down the mountain. He came to rest in a spot so treacherous that the recovery team deemed it inaccessible. He lies there yet, high on the mountain's north face, amid the beauty and the bittersweet of the summing up which he, like all of us, selected for his own.

I went home, content with my decision. I would not stop going to the mountains; I could never do that. But my adventures now would be gentle ones—bright rambles up rounded slopes, where a slip might result in a twisted ankle but never a broken neck. I vowed that I would learn to be content with the tranquillity of the meadows, streams, and forests I had so often hurried past in my quest for the solitude of the summits.

A few weeks later I returned again to Pennsylvania, where late one night my father, perhaps carrying out an unconscious decision of his own, had been taken by ambulance to the local hospital. When I arrived he had been moved to the intensive care unit and there connected to the bewildering implements of survival which, unlike the rope of the mountaineer, we have come to fear so much.

Through the long hours at my father's bedside I did not pray that he would recover. I told him in a steady voice that if he wanted to die I understood, and that he had my blessing. As he slowly slipped away I was happy simply to hold his hand and to stroke his head, and to let him know that he was loved. I let go at last, and on the third morning he did the same, setting off on a voyage to a strange and enchanting world that I did not fear, that I knew to be peaceful and generous and good.

Among the mythologies of the world no theme is more persistent than that of the interdependence of love and death. On the Indonesian island of West Ceram they tell of the murder of the maiden Hainuwele and how, because of her death, both plants and sexual organs came into the world. The Ojibway of Lake Superior believe that the Great Spirit allowed his angel Mondawmin to die in order that Indians might have maize; Christians hold a similar belief involving God's beloved son and a gift of eternal life. So enduring is the motif that we must ask ourselves whether love and death, like Nirvana and the summit, may not be one and the same—neither beginning nor end, neither process nor experience nor condition of any kind, but a means through which we share in that universal and boundless energy we call nature. A year has passed and now the dazzling clarity of late summer has come to the mountains of New Mexico. Under a sky of incandescent blue, Carol and I wander upward among the breathtaking pinnacles of the San-dias, a rock climber's paradise just a stone's throw from where we live. On this quiet afternoon we have given ourselves over to reverie; Carol is lost in thought, while I speculate on pine cones, bumblebees, and, most of all, the baby of whom we have begun to dream.

Across the canyon a tower called the Pulpit rises suddenly into view. The shock is stunning. Unable to resist, I am tossed violently into the past: I stop, rivet my eyes on the face, scan it minutely for the route, the way, the edge, the last dance on thin air . . .

The slip lasts only a moment. Then Carol and I fall into step and re-sume our gentle stroll.

The Trail
to the
Westering Sea

*All history consists of successive excursions from a
single starting-point, to which man returns again
and again to organize another search for a durable
scale of values.*

ALDO LEOPOLD, *A Sand County Almanac*

I

It is October and I go to the mountain.

Low in the sky a crescent moon dips toward the distant ridge. Idle
morning, clear and silent, drifts on a warm wind across the dry sagebrush flats of eastern California. Before me a narrow dirt road leads
west toward the mountain. The road is my link with the past, my path-
way into history.

When I was young I lived in a small town set among the fine hard-
wood forests of northwestern Pennsylvania. That region of rolling hills
inspired a taste in landscapes that favored the graceful over the vertical.

Not surprisingly, the mountain generated little enthusiasm among the people who lived in my town.

But October—electrifying October!—was a different matter: a beloved rite, a celebration of life, a pulse-quickening community dance during which we tossed aside our cares like paper cups and kicked up our heels with joy. In the familiar orange of aging maple leaves we found the bearings we had lost in pointless summer. October was our reference point, our flooding of the Nile. As the season turned we saw confirmed the laws of nature and learned the fundamental truth contained in circles. A pattern emerged, and with it a reason to begin again.

At other times of the year my neighbors sometimes spoke wistfully of October as though it were a fond friend off dallying on a slow trip around the world. Then fall came home and the hillsides ran wild with color. Those were golden and simple and splendid days; they filled me with a sense of excitement about living I have never experienced since. October was scored onto my soul like initials on a tree. Other enchantments would come and go, but the first one would remain with me always.

In California, autumn inspires no such soaring of the spirit. Here nature's gifts arrive almost daily, and in that embarrassment of riches no month or season outshines the rest. But ahead of me, along the east side of the mountain, it is sometimes possible to find a trace of that soul-scoring image of October. There on a fall day like today, cottonwood and aspen sometimes flame orange and yellow beside a mountain stream. It's not the whole truth but it's a start . . . and a start is what I'm after as I head upward to make contact with another Pennsylvanian, and with an October as distant and faded as the waning moon.

His name was Zenas Leonard, and he passed this way when California was still a land where padres tended missions and brown-eyed señoritas twirled parasols while strolling on their evening promenades. Leonard hailed from Clearfield, Pennsylvania; like me, he went west at a certain moment in his life, and so grew to appreciate the vertical as

well as the graceful. He became a mountain man—in Bernard De-
Voto's apt figure, a hickory knot. He walked to these pale sagebrush flats
from Clearfield by way of terra incognita, straddling the ends of the
earth. It was a mountain man's lark he was on: he wanted to see the Pacific. Near Willow Springs, California, I've picked up his trail, beside
a feeder stream of the East Walker River. I've come to follow him on a
grand and brave adventure, a mountain man's lark of my own—along
the stream, through the forest, up the mountain, over the top, and, if
we're lucky, down the opposite side.

The road creaks over a rickety bridge. The sun arches higher. The
moon curves under the sea. I read from the *Narrative of the Adventures
of Zenas Leonard*: "The next day we travelled up this river towards the
mountain, where we encamped for the night. This mountain is very
high, as the snow extends down the side nearly half way . . ."

Two lapsed Pennsylvanians in the heart of the West, off for a tilt at
the mountain—the range a Franciscan missionary once called *una
gran sierra nevada*.

The year was 1833. Andrew Jackson had just begun his second term as
president of a nation that now comprised twenty-four states. The
Cumberland Road, highway of the pioneers, pushed inland all the
way to Columbus, Ohio. In midsummer a settlement of forty-three
houses and two hundred people was incorporated on the shores of Lake
Michigan as the village of Chicago. America's reach was westward,
though her grasp as yet extended no further than Missouri. St. Louis
was still a frontier town, Fort Leavenworth on the Missouri River the
last outpost of civilization. Anyone who set off into the wilderness beyond could have no more certainty about the outcome than might have
been mustered for a trip to Cathay six hundred years earlier. In the untamed West, "nothing was heard from dark to day light but the fierce
and terrifying growls of wild beasts," wrote Zenas Leonard, who had
reason to know, "and the more shrill cries of the merciless savages."

In the spring of 1830 Leonard left Pennsylvania to work as a trapper in the Rocky Mountains. He reached St. Louis the following year and signed on with the fur-trading firm of Gantt and Blackwell. In April 1831 his employer sent him and a company of sixty-nine other wide-eyed speculators in beaver futures up the Missouri to fur country. Leonard was twenty-two years old, off to make his way in the world as a purveyor of pelts to grace the hats of gentlemen; or, as he might have put it, as a skinner of flat tails.

By 1833 Gantt and Blackwell had gone bankrupt and Leonard had gained some insight into both the ways of the world and beaver futures. During one nine-day stretch on the way west he had subsisted on nothing but dried beaver skins. As a recipient of the customary measure of misadventure he had battled thirst, freezing cold, and unmerciful heat, and had barely escaped death in a bloody clash with Gros Ventres Indians that cost several trappers their lives.

In July, Leonard and the disgruntled survivors of his outfit joined several hundred other veterans of the skin game and an equal number of Indians beside Horse Creek, a tributary of Wyoming's Green River. The occasion was the annual fur trappers' rendezvous. Here the men traded off the pelts they had collected during a year in the wild and re-supplied for another year, courtesy of caravans sent out from the East by the fur companies. The crowning feature of the rendezvous, however, was not economic but social, the opportunity it provided for the trappers to catch up on diversions that had been missing from their lives: guzzling gallon jugs of a vile concoction called skull varnish, debauching dusk to dawn with genial Snake and Nez Percé Indian women, and gouging each other's eyes out. The rendezvous was heaven. Punctuating the revelry were shooting matches and horse races, gambling games and duels, wrestling matches, drunken brawls, and now and then a cold-blooded murder.

In their weakened condition trappers willingly paid astronomical prices for supplies. Markups ran as high as 2,000 percent. By late July most of the men were in hock up to their powder horns and had signed over to their creditors some or all of their pelts for the following year.

The company agents then headed east to count the profits while the trappers fanned out over the Rockies to work the streams for several months before the freeze set in. Through the winter each man holed up in a skin lodge somewhere deep in the mountains. To help him through the cold winter nights he sometimes kept with him an Indian woman he had purchased at the rendezvous. The dreamers among them lived on sustaining visions of new horizons to set out for one year—Mexico or Oregon or, for Zenas Leonard, the wide blue ocean at the end of the West.

The golden years of the fur trade passed swiftly. Only sixteen rendezvous were held, the last in 1840. The tastes of gentlemen began to run to lacquered silk, and beaver hats fell out of fashion. In 1833, the year of the Horse Creek rendezvous, the bottom dropped out of the market. Beaver pelts that had sold for $6 a pound on the St. Louis market a year earlier now went for $3.50 a pound or less.

Even had the fashion not changed, it is unlikely that the fur companies could have continued to supply the hat manufacturers. After a decade of intensive trapping, the Rocky Mountain streams had nearly been trapped out. Mountain men found themselves ranging farther and farther afield in their quest for pelts. For the first time, a group of Americans faced a preposterous abolition of their God-given right to exploit the land. Simply put, they had used up the beaver.

With Gantt and Blackwell out of the picture, Leonard went looking for a new employer. He found one in Captain Benjamin Bonneville, an army officer organizing a search for new sources of fur in the unexplored country west of the Great Salt Lake. To Leonard, this meant Far West. "I was anxious to go to the coast of the Pacific," he wrote, and eagerly signed on with the expedition. Because he possessed "a common English education" and "strong mental faculties"—real rarities at the rendezvous—Leonard was appointed clerk of the expedition.

To lead the party Bonneville chose a neck-or-nothing Tennessean named Joe Walker, a professional tumbleweed who, according to one admiring colleague, "didn't follow trails but made them." Late in July 1833, as the Horse Creek rendezvous staggered to a close, Walker bid goodbye to Bonneville and, with fifty-seven bleary-eyed trappers and some two hundred horses behind him, headed downstream. Before him lay the Utah salt flats, the Nevada desert, the dry valley of the Humboldt, and—seven hundred miles away, near today's settlement of Willow Springs, California—the towering Sierra Nevada.

It's doubtful that Bonneville instructed Walker to hike all the way to California. But the Tennessee rambler had a tendency toward reck-lessness. Moreover, in wide-open country he relied on a recalcitrant inner compass that jabbed annoyingly at his spirit whenever he tried to change directions. Two months later he and his men walked out of the desert into eastern California. Then they set off on a rash attempt to do something that had never before been done by white men: to cross the mountains that were blocking their way west (thoroughly dispiriting Walker), the mountains known today as the High Sierra.

A century and a half later I have come here for the same reason. I want to retrace Walker's route over the mountains. I want to see the country he saw. With Zenas Leonard's journal to guide me, I want to stop in my tracks and turn back to an earlier time, to view the Sierra as the expedition clerk had, as unknown country glistening with the dew of creation.

Unlike most other sports, mountain walking and climbing allow one to relive great events of the past very much as they were originally experienced. The ordinary tennis player can never square off against Martina Navratilova at Wimbledon, but a climber today can follow Hillary's and Tenzing's footsteps to the summit of Everest, or—a less lofty example—John Muir's to the top of Mount Ritter; or a hiker can retrace Robert Marshall's path through Alaska's Brooks Range, under the same conditions and in need of the same skills and physical strength as were originally required.

Of course, those who prefer to make history rather than recreate it will point out that people who follow footsteps never get anywhere, except perhaps lost in the crowd. They take as their model Robert Scott, who said he enjoyed traipsing off into the unknown because of his fascination with making the first footprints. What they forget, but I do not, is that one of Scott's first footprints was also his last. Thus my dogged preference for second and third footprints.

The wisdom of this prudent approach to exploration is underscored by the example of a New Hampshire man I once knew. An inveterate mountain walker, he had wandered the wilds of New England ever since he was a boy. In sixty-odd years of such rambles he had never once had an accident.

My friend explained to me that he always owned a hound of one kind or another, and that he always granted the privilege of going first in the woods to the dog. If the two of them came to a log, the dog went over first; if there was a stream to be waded, the dog got the honors. Each time, if the dog made out all right the man followed. This technique of wilderness survival is hard on dogs but easy on people. My friend lived to a ripe old age.

I don't know what it was that drew that gracious man into the woods year after year; for me, part of the lure is what Aldo Leopold called "a love for what was," a desire "to see America as history, to conceive of destiny as a becoming, to smell a hickory tree through the still lapse of ages." To love what was (which is different from merely feeling nostalgic) is not high on the current list of fashionable things to do. Nevertheless, it is true: I carry a torch for the grizzlies that once roamed the California mountains; I long for the wolves that loped over the Great Plains; I'm enchanted by the long-vanished forest that stretched uninterrupted from the Appalachians to the Mississippi, an infinity of hardwoods, thick as a jungle. How wonderful that jungle was! Imagine if you can: a squirrel could climb a tree in the Carolinas and scamper all the way to Illinois without once touching the ground. The possibility of such a flight was a greater miracle than anything NASA will ever achieve.

I think it's a love for what was that makes winter in the mountains so captivating for me. From a lookout on a high ridge I see the world buried beneath the snow, looking just as it did fifty, a hundred, a million years ago. No roads or power lines are visible. The cold air shines like polished crystal. The scene is simple, a seed lying dormant: it resonates with potential, yet it's unhurried, content with the present. I sense a purity and interconnectedness of things that in other seasons and from other viewpoints escape me.

Even when the snow is gone, I can sometimes catch the vanishing odor of Leopold's fallen hickory tree by going to the site of its interment and pausing there to honor the memory of the richness and the fullness of its life. In doing so I have faith that something meaningful will result—some enlightenment, a flash of insight. A trip to a hickory tree or to a mountain can be many things: an opportunity to study, or to play, or to prove one's courage. For me it is often something like a trip to a museum. I wander over mountain meadows and up snowfields, taking in the sights as though they were Etruscan vases. A pioneer trail or a classic climbing route is a gift from the past, an opportunity to share in the making of history. By walking the trail or climbing the route I accept the gift. My journey becomes a cultural act, an embracing of my heritage.

In turn it gives me something of my own to share. By going to the mountain I take my part in a time-honored ritual. The circle is joined. I too become history.

II

I have been hiking alone for five days. My ramble began in Mammoth Lakes, California, and has taken me fifty miles up the east side of the Sierra, along dirt roads and mountain trails to this stream near Willow Springs, a speck of ink on the map not far from the village of Bridgeport: a slow northering to meet Walker coming in from Nevada. From here I'll turn southwest and for another fifty miles or so follow Walker's route, as closely as I can determine it, up and over the spine of the

Sierra and down to my final destination, a bus station in Yosemite Valley.

The morning air is tart with the melancholy aroma of sage. It's a good smell to accompany a walk into the past. Behind me some low hills hide a cirque that my map identifies as Big Alkali. A hideous name, to be sure, but one that brilliantly conveys the sense of the desert country that sits dull as lard east of the Sierra.

In October 1833, Joe Walker and a somewhat chastened party of trappers arrived here from over near Big Alkali. The journey from the Great Salt Lake had been a nightmare. For much of it they had followed the Humboldt River, which for reasons only someone on intimate terms with the Nevada landscape could understand they called the Barren River. Uncertainty over the intentions of the local Indians had plagued the trappers for days at a time. Most western tribes, according to passing diarists, manifested one or two redeeming features. But those who hit Nevada pronounced the Indians there despicable—totally uncivilized.

"They are generally small and weak, and some of them very hairy," wrote Leonard in the closest he came to a compliment. Several decades later Mark Twain was less generous: the "wretchedest type of mankind I have ever seen," he called them. Even the usually tolerant John Muir had a hard time with the desert Indians. Once he met a group of them near Mono Lake. "The dirt on their faces was fairly stratified," he observed with his keen scientific eye, "and seemed so ancient and so undisturbed it might almost possess a geological significance."

In the light of a later day we have seen that the native peoples of the region were neither warlike nor uncivilized—quite the opposite. Walker and his men, however, felt badgered. Everywhere they looked they saw savages peering at them through the rabbit brush. At night the Indians sang and danced near their camps—clear preparations for attack. At last the tension boiled over. Rifles blaring, thirty-two of the trappers waded into a party of Indians, killing thirty-nine of them.

But if Indians had been easy to locate, the same could not be said of food. The desert had contained little game, and the expedition's supply of dried buffalo meat was nearly exhausted. The horses, having found little forage, were on the verge of starvation. Ironically, there had also been almost no beaver, leaving the men to ponder what they were doing in that no-man's land. Now they faced the unwelcome challenge of crossing a range of high mountains, where winter was waiting sure as skull varnish to ambush them at the pass.

I greet Walker and the boys with a tip of my green felt hat. Then I hoist my backpack into the air—fifty-five pounds, much of it extra food and cold-weather gear to save my skin should a storm hit during the next few days. I mate sluggishly with the shoulder straps of my pack, then stumble off up the road as though I were wearing a piano.

I don't know where Walker headed up over the Sierra; no one does. From the few details of the journey that Leonard entered in his journal, people who puzzle over this sort of thing have determined that the route lies somewhere within a few miles on either side of me. Walker had to have followed a stream upward to a pass on the crest of the range. That narrows the list of possible routes to half a dozen. I've ruled out the passes to the north, which are surrounded by an array of sharp granite spires called the Sawtooth Ridge. They appear insurmountable; Walker wouldn't have gone that way.

To the south lies easier country than Leonard described. So his route lies straight ahead somewhere. But several creeks rise in the mountains ahead. Which one could it be?

With fifty-five pounds bearing down on me, the thought of taking off cross-country toward some promising but remote mountain stream never enters my mind. I'll follow the dirt road, which dissolves in Green Creek Canyon ten miles ahead. On the horizon before me I see the two ridges that tower above Green Creek, and a broad cut on the skyline between them. It suddenly looks like a perfectly sensible route. Walker, of course, didn't have the dirt road, but I do, and without a second thought I cast my lot with Green Creek.

At an altitude of around seven thousand feet the road begins to rise sharply. Ahead the peaks grow larger. The Sierra Nevada: the biggest single chunk of mountain scenery in the country. Rising in the north near volcanic Mount Lassen, the range runs more than four hundred miles to Tehachapi Pass, unbroken by a river along its entire length. The southern half of the uplift, one section of which I'm approaching, is the scenic climax of the range—the High Sierra. It's the center for mountaineering and tourism, the site of three national parks (Yosemite, Sequoia, and Kings Canyon) and half a dozen federal wilderness areas.

Because of the protected status of much of the High Sierra, a visitor today can see the range more or less as it appeared to Joe Walker. Naturally, changes have taken place. Trails now crisscross the back country. Cattle graze at the lower elevations. Mines, ski developments, and vacation cabins encircle the range. The Tioga Road traverses the crest, intersecting Walker's route. But most of the major development has occurred along the periphery; once inside, the back-country traveler can roam freely over a huge region that has not been greatly altered by humans. Where significant changes were wrought in the past— mountainsides logged over, meadows overgrazed—slow recovery has begun. The hiker glimpses what Robinson Jeffers meant by "the extraordinary patience of things," how "the image of the pristine beauty lives in the very grain of the granite."

The changes wrought by nature are all but imperceptible. In the century and a half since Walker passed this way, the crest of the range above Willow Springs has risen just a foot or so. The winter wind that roars down Green Creek Canyon is about as savage today as it was in 1833. The evergreen trees that line the canyon are as green as ever. Cataclysms such as forest fires or avalanches have dramatically altered the face of the range from time to time, but the mountain soon recovers from the shock. In a few decades only a trained naturalist will perceive that here occurred a brief interruption in the plodding course of events—an avalanche, a falling leaf.

Until the nineteenth century the Sierra was an enigma to the white settlers of the region, a barrier both to travel and to a full understanding of the geography of the West. As late as 1817, thrilling rumors circulated among Spanish missionaries in California that on the far side of the Sierra *people* could be found, people "like our soldiers." Whether these creatures were Spanish, English, or something else altogether was a matter for only the wildest speculation. So too was the perplexing question of whether it was Texas or Oregon (or, for that matter, Zanzibar) that lay beyond the snowy peaks.

Then in what was for those days lightning succession, the first two steps toward solving the mysteries of the Sierra were taken. In the spring of 1827, Jed Smith, Silas Gobel, and Robert Evans pushed through the north end of the range near Ebbetts Pass. It was rugged country, but at less than nine thousand feet in elevation it hardly posed the dangers they would have faced in the High Sierra.

Smith, Gobel, and Evans crossed the range from west to east. Six years later Walker arrived to test the High Sierra in the opposite direction, my direction. Weary beneath my pack, watching my steps, still I lift my head listlessly from time to time to check the view ahead. A rabble of clouds begins to gather above the peaks. Details are sharpening—rocky ridges, steep faces split by dark, ominous cracks. Slopes that looked easy to climb are overcoming the illusions of distance, and the ascent to the crest starts to look hard. I'd like the mountains at least to be beautiful but they are not. Soon, after the first snowfall, the view from here will be spectacular, with the peaks sparkling like mica; now they are bare, brown as bran muffins.

The dirt road traverses the side of a hill. It rounds a corner and suddenly enters the narrow valley of Green Creek. A burst of color startles me. Beside the creek, a solar flare has been unleashed. Aspen trees ablaze in October yellow, orange, and red shimmer beside the water. Feeling a rush of excitement, I stop and face the stream. The sight is glorious; for a moment I'm transfixed. I look farther up the canyon and my heart leaps at the sight of a lush cascade of yellow pouring toward me. Then something strange happens: for an instant I smell burning leaves. I haven't smelled that acid odor for years but I recognize it at once. In a moment it is gone.

On October days decades ago, huge piles of oak and maple leaves burned in the streets and backyards of my hometown in Pennsylvania. Columns of gray smoke rose toward the sky like geysers, and for weeks the scent of burning leaves pervaded the town. Once, in a gesture laden with goodwill, my brain tucked away the formula for the smell of burning leaves among the ganglia that cluster in the far reaches of my subconscious. Today the conditions were right, and the neurological remains of a cloud of smoke were vented at last.

"To smell a hickory tree through the still lapse of ages . . ."

The part memory plays in creating the pleasure mountains give me had not occurred to me before. My trips into the high country have seemed to grow more enjoyable year by year, as though each time I built on the accumulated pleasures of the past. Even when it isn't stirring me with a palpable sensation like long-forgotten smoke, could my teeming subconscious be calling up subliminal sensations—single-frame memories—from my ever-expanding stock, and then firing them away at my pleasure centers like buckshot?

Someone has suggested that thrill-seekers do what they do because they are addicted to adrenaline. Perhaps I do what I do, go to the mountain, because I am addicted to the dazzling kaleidoscope of revealed memories that the mountain induces in me. Crafty female moths and monkeys (and maybe even humans) spray pheromones over the countryside. These tiny aphrodisiacs, only eight or ten carbon atoms in length, are powerful enough to waylay every male of the species for miles around and send him dancing into the boudoir. If moths and monkeys can let fly with pheromones, then why not mountains?

But why stop there—why not oceans and lakes and fishing holes and prairies and the arctic, and every other place that stirs our imaginations and compels us irresistibly in its direction? Nature beckons, and all of us, each in our own way, give in to the call. But is there more than memory behind our surrender? Sometimes my longing to be in the mountains is so urgent it seems that only instinct could be responsible—a yearning rooted in some random, outrageous, splendid accident of genetic mutation suffered eons ago by some ancestor of mine.

Imagine: the bollixed chromosome gave rise to a creature that enjoyed wandering over hill and dale, it knew not why; and, what is more amazing, that thereby gained a selective advantage over others of its species. The restless gene prospered during the long, uncompromising march of evolution, residing in a line of happy wanderers that led unswervingly to my birthplace. If the scenario is accurate, the gene is in me yet, constraining me to fulfill some inscrutable purpose beyond my understanding.

The thought is haunting. Is the freedom of the hills an illusion? When I go to the mountain, am I no freer than a bird nesting in spring, or a salmon swimming home?

The road levels out along the creek. My spirits are soaring. Lodgepole pine mingles with the aspen, and farther up the canyon a softwood forest is beginning to come into focus. I check my topo map, a confidence-inspiring tool not available to Joe Walker. He may have had a map, yes, but not one likely to have inspired confidence. The best map then in circulation demanded of its owner mostly a robust sense of humor. It featured several nonexistent rivers, a chain of Rocky Mountains eight hundred miles wide, and no Sierra at all. Most travelers found they were better off without it.

Given the half-baked geographical information available to Walker, it is entirely possible that the Sierra, rising directly in his path, came as a surprise to him. Certainly he could have had no idea how far it was to the other side of the range. But Walker, wrote Zenas Leonard, was "a man who was seldom mistaken in anything he undertook." He was not about to turn around and head back across the terrible Nevada moonscape. His food supplies were running out and the mountainsides ahead probably harbored game.

Besides, in a day or two they might be over the top. Then it would be all downhill to that lazy blue ocean they had been dreaming about for weeks, and those bottomless kegs of sweet California brandy; and best of all (in each man's most persistent dream), to a honey-brown woman with dark shining eyes, a well-turned figure, and a foolish craving to sit rapt and open-lipped while a whiskered mountain man told her what it was like to ride a horse through hell.

Walker was keen to get on with it.

In the morning we despatched hunters to the mountain on search of game and also to look out for a pass over the mountain, as our provisions were getting scarce—our dried buffaloe meat being almost done. After prowling about all day, our hunters returned in the evening, bringing the unwelcome tidings that they had not seen any signs of game in all their ramblings, and what was equally discouraging, that they had seen no practicable place for crossing the mountain.

"The mountain"? Where was it?

It was everywhere. The mountain Leonard wrote of was not a specific peak, but the entire chain of peaks that blocked the way west. Throughout his narrative the expedition clerk referred to the Sierra as "the mountain." Not once did he dream up a descriptive or fanciful name for some feature of the range, as many have done since. It may have been that such an act of whimsy, or intimacy, was impossible while the Sierra posed a threat to his life. By lumping the peaks together as "the mountain," Leonard was defining his relationship with the opposition (unfriendly, suspicious, fearful), in the same way a soldier lumps human beings together as "the enemy" to define his.

By contrast, I have ahead of me a landscape as exhaustively named as the contents of a Whitman's Sampler. Kavanaugh Ridge rises to my left, Monument Ridge to my right. Page, Gabbro, Epidote, and Dunderberg peaks stand high above my route, and a chain of lakes— Green, East, Nutter, Gilman, Hoover, Summit—line its side. Knowing that these features have names, have been visited before, eases some of my fears about crossing the Sierra with winter approaching; it imparts on these surroundings a vague sense of benevolence Leonard could never have known.

Nor did I expect to have to fight the Indians. Out searching for a path over the mountain, Walker and Leonard flushed two Indians out of hiding. Terrified, the two tried to escape. They dashed at a scout named George Nidever, who thought they were attacking him. Nidever raised his rifle and fired point-blank into the Indians. The shot tore through the first man and buried itself deep in the second. Both men died instantly.

"Mr. Nidever was very sorry when he discovered what he had done," reported Leonard.

At last one of the scouts came across an apparent Indian trail leading west. The entire party moved to trailside, and each man readied himself for the journey up and over the mountain the following morning.

III

Green Lake. Size: half a mile long, a quarter-mile wide. Setting: a steep-sided bowl scooped from the base of Gabbro Peak, a few hundred yards below tree line in Toiyabe National Forest. Elevation: just under nine thousand feet. Population: one.

By midafternoon I had reached the end of the dirt road, where the Forest Service maintains a small public campground. No one was there. No one is anywhere today. After six days of hiking alone I'm aching for companionship. From the campground I hiked two miles to Green Lake along a wide, well-maintained trail. From the highway twelve miles behind me to Summit Pass, five miles ahead, no one is following in Joe Walker's footsteps today but me.

Late in the afternoon the wind shifts. Above, the clouds are in turmoil and the sky darkens. Thunder rumbles behind a ridge. A front is moving in, and rain—snow, if the temperature drops a few degrees— is on the way.

I drop my pack and scour the lakeside in search of a camping spot.

An old fear of getting wet in the mountains wells up in me. I scrounge about in the trees, along the shore, above the trail in the rocks. Finally, on a rise overlooking the lake I spot a tightly knit stand of lodgepole pines with just enough space between them for a body. It will do.

Moments after I crawl into my bivouac sack the sky opens. A torrent of rain pours down on me and tears at my protective cover. I lie stunned in the dark, the waterproof material pressing cold and hard against my face. I can hear the wind screaming down the canyon, the rain rudely slapping my body. I am in the midst of all this, foolish, mad perhaps, lost in a premonition of catastrophe. My distress is so great that when the canyon suddenly grows quiet, I draw, not the happy conclusion that the rain has stopped, but the alarming one that it has begun to snow.

But I am wrong. Perhaps an hour after the start of the storm I peer out of my cocoon for the first time. It looks miserable outside, but above me a few openings have appeared in the clouds. If the weather is like this tomorrow, shall I continue? Once over the pass I'll be in Virginia Canyon, in the outback of Yosemite. I've seen Virginia Canyon from the summit of Mount Hoffmann fifteen miles away and it looked delightful; now it sounds frightening. Marooned on the far side of the pass, miles from the nearest highway, cut off by a snowstorm—I'd be in a jam. I begin to wish that a blizzard would hit right now. My decision would be made for me. In the morning I'd stumble down to the highway and go home.

I write in my journal: "I'm alone at the lake, I think. I'm anxious about the weather, a little scared. Zenas had it worse, of course, but at least he had fifty-seven companions."

As darkness falls, my loneliness and my terrible sense of isolation in this canyon combine to extract their toll: the serenity of the wild Sierra crashes in my head, and I am overcome by a profound foreboding.

I slip from my bivouac sack and in my bare feet begin prowling the lake shore in search of help. The clouds part briefly; golden shafts of light from the dying sun strike the water. The air around me suddenly thickens with an eerie, shimmering glow. An unearthly quiet fills the canyon. I have the strong impression that another person is nearby.

Quickly now, I drop into a gully, then mount some boulders to a viewpoint on the opposite side. Straining my eyes in the half-light, I look toward distant, scarcely visible trees. And then I spot it: a large orange tarp, strung from the trees to protect someone—perhaps several people!—from the rain.

I hurry toward them through the falling night, my eyes fixed on the tarp. My feet are wet and very cold. As I approach the camp I become disoriented in the strange light. I stop and squint at the tarp. My head is spinning. Suddenly the orange shape begins to disintegrate. As I watch without comprehending, it resolves into a million tiny pieces, like a microscope slide coming gradually into focus.

The tree is dazzling. It is an aspen. Its orange leaves glow in the dense twilight before me, like slowly dying embers.

IV

Leonard described the climb to the crest of the Sierra:

> In the morning we started on our toilsome journey. Ascending the mountain we found to be very difficult from the rocks and its steepness. This day we made but poor speed, and encamped on the side of the mountain. . . . Continued our course until in the afternoon, when we arrived at what we took for the top, where we again camped, but without any thing to eat for our horses, as the ground was covered with a deep snow, which from appearance, lays on the North side of the peaks, the whole year around. These peaks are totally covered with rocks and sand, —totally incapable of vegetation; except on the South side, where grows a kind of Juniper or Gin shrub, bearing a berry tasting similar to gin. Here we passed the night without anything to eat except these gin berries, and some of the insects from the lake described above, which our men had got from the Indians. We had not suffered much

from cold for several months previous to this; but this night, surrounded as we were with the everlasting snows on the summit of this
mountain, the cold was felt with three fold severity.

At the crest the party passed over a broad saddle more than ten thousand feet above sea level. They were nearly two thousand feet higher
than Jed Smith had been at the highest point of his crossing six years
earlier.

The pass was undistinguished. A few weatherworn whitebark pines
were scattered on the ridge. Left and right scree slopes swept upward,
moderately at first, then more and more steeply; far above the pass,
each slope solidified into massive gray blocks before topping out at the
summit of a twelve-thousand-foot peak.

Walker might have dreamed of standing at the pass and looking out
toward a hazy sky-blue ocean; instead, he gazed westward into a wasteland of rock and snow that stretched to the horizon. Tall peaks rose up
on all sides; dark, forested valleys wound among the peaks, cruel walk-
ways through a maze. If there was an ocean, it was hidden far beyond
this shapeless wilderness.

The next morning it was with no cheerful prospect that each man prepared himself for travelling, as we had nothing to eat worth mentioning. As we advanced, in the hollows sometimes we would encounter
prodigious quantities of snow. When we would come to such places, a
certain portion of the men would be appointed alternately to go forward
and break the road, to enable our horses to get through; and if any of the
horses would get swamped, these same men were to get them out. In
this tedious and tiresome manner we spent the whole day without going
more than 8 or 10 miles. In some of these ravines where the snow is
drifted from the peaks, it never entirely melts, and may be found at this
season of the year, from ten to one hundred feet deep.

Reading Leonard's story, it is easy to begin to feel sorry for these miserable wretches floundering through the snow. Leonard, I think,
would defiantly have refused any such sympathy. These were not in-

nocent emigrants caught in a surprise snowstorm; they were mountain men, professional adventurers fiercely proud of their calling. If from time to time their derring-do left them out on a rotten limb, their wilderness savvy would probably save them. If it didn't, they would go down without a grumble.

The romantic legend of the mountain man hides the stark truth that the freedom he enjoyed—a freedom unsurpassed in our history—was attained at the expense of the forward march of civilization. Mountain men were Huns. They took what they wanted and left what they didn't. If luck was with them they feasted on buffalo liver, tongue, and hump ribs; if it wasn't they turned without flinching to ants, tree bark, crickets, moccasins, and Indians' flesh. They fought for sport and killed with abandon. They died with abandon, too. Not many more than a thousand mountain men in all worked the streams of the Rockies during the great years of the fur trade. Two hundred were killed by Indians. Hundreds more were killed by wild animals, starvation, freezing weather, and drowning. A few were done in by their own companions. Death became as real to the mountain man as life, and he accorded each a degree of composure that bordered on apathy. Joe Meek, one of Leonard's companions on the Sierra crossing, once came upon four fellow trappers playing cards. A fifth man was in the game, in a way— dead, serving as the card table.

"Habitual watchfulness destroys every frivolity of mind and action," wrote mountain man Tom Farnham of his comrades.

They seldom smile: the expression of their countenances is watchful, solemn, and determined. They ride and walk like men whose breasts have so long been exposed to the bullet and the arrow, that fear finds within them no resting place.

But who can fault their motives? There was money to be made adventuring, of course, but not much; most of it was probably squandered at the rendezvous. A few men went to the Rockies to escape from the law; a few, from domestic problems at home. But for many it was the beauty and the freedom of the wilderness that drew them into the unknown West. Leonard wrote of the plains that bordered the Missouri River:

> We found the country here beautiful indeed—abounding with the most delightful prairies, with here and there a small brook, winding its way to the river, the margins of which are adorned with the lofty Pine and Cedar tree. These prairies were completely covered with fine low grass, and decorated with beautiful flowers of various colors; and some of them are so extensive and clear of timber and brush that the eye might search in vain for an object to rest upon. I have seen beautiful and enchanting sceneries depicted by the artist, but never anything to equal the work of rude nature in those prairies. In the spring of the year when the grass is green and the blossoms fresh, they present an appearance, which for beauty and charms, is beyond the art of man to depict.

At night camaraderie awaited them by the campfire:

> These men killed ten Buffaloe, from which they selected one of the fattest humps they could find and brought in, and after roasting it handsomely before the fire, we all seated ourselves upon the ground, encircling, what we there called a splendid repast to dine upon. Feasting sumptuously, cracking a few jokes, taking a few rounds with our rifles, and wishing heartily for some liquor . . .

It's a compelling picture: a cluster of men, bearded, buckskin-clad, seated by a fire flaming orange on the vast prairie. The smoke billows up. The coals sparkle and flare and now, on a rise overlooking Green Lake, glow beside me in the night. The wind howls and I am restless. Sleep comes for only minutes at a time.

A journey into the wilderness is a reenactment of the whole of the westward movement, run in reverse, and I am well along in the drama. A complete performance goes something like this: you exit from a modern car and hike along a dirt road built in the 1950s to a CCC trail cut in the thirties. If you have companions, conversation simplifies, culture slips to the level of whistling or recitations of Robert Service poems. Jobs grow more physical, the privy less private. Specialization disappears and chores are shared. Class distinctions moderate. You nibble on berries and perch on rocks. In the wind and the trees, you seek spirits and sometimes find them. You find camaraderie beside the campfire. In the final scene—or is it the first?—you lie awake on the hard ground, tormented by primitive fears of thunder and the black of night.

Dawn. An uneasy calm envelops peak and canyon and lakeside as from each, one by one, the darkness is drawn away. The eastern sky flares wild and crimson. At the north end of Green Lake I reach for my canteen and discover that the water in it has turned to ice.

My heart sinks. I turn over and consider going back to sleep. But it's not a real option. Slowly and without enthusiasm I wriggle from my sleeping bag.

Not long after I rise my mood improves. As I eat breakfast I search the western sky and pretend to read signs of clearing in the dense collage of grays. I realize that I want badly to go on—and the decision is made. I pull on my pack and head for the pass.

The trail snakes upward past several lakes where ice clear and delicate as damselfly wings tightens the surfaces of shallow backwashes. I trudge on, uneasy at the realization that the morning is unfolding as gloomily as I had feared.

But, as I continue, a sense of adventure takes hold. I begin to see in the moist earth of the path ahead and the mist of the upper canyon, not sources of concern, but fresh, unexpected, exciting sights. My senses awaken. I marvel at a thick cushion of moss, so green and full of energy it appears ready to burst. The urgent melody of a nearby brook brightens my step. Just as they did yesterday, my spirits lift when I look outside myself.

Soon I reach timberline. Above the pass the sky is a gray wash. Yellow stump grass replaces the evergreen of the lower canyon. Rust-streaked boulders pepper the trailside. The wind whips my parka and I stop to pull on woolen mittens. For two hours I move steadily upward, firmly committed now to completing my journey.

At its head the canyon opens out into a jumble of rocks and trickling streams. Then I mount a final rise, skirt one last lonely lake, and I'm there: Summit Pass on the crest of the Sierra, the unguarded entrance to Yosemite National Park and the high point of my trip.

I let out a great shout of joy. My voice ricochets among the steep walls of the nearby peaks. In my notebook I scribble: "Hooray! (So far.)"

A few flakes of snow twinkle aimlessly in the thin air. I linger just long enough to catch a few of the fatter specimens in the palm of my hand, then charge down the steep trail that will take me into the heart of Virginia Canyon.

Within minutes a remarkable change comes over the Yosemite high country. The air grows still. In the overcast above me, odd-shaped patches of blue open like wildflowers. Suddenly a spotlight of sun illuminates the forest ahead. It is a miracle. I gaze in astonishment for a moment, then take off running down the trail—

For the Walker party there was no running down a trail. They plodded along through deep snow, now dragging starving horses behind them. Leonard's journal begins to focus on the terrible ordeal of the horses.

"This day's travel was very severe on our horses, as they had not a particle to eat. They began to grow stupid and stiff, and we began to despair of getting them over the mountain."

That evening: "Two of our horses were so much reduced that it was thought they would not be able to travel in the morning at all, whereupon it was agreed that they should be butchered for the use of the men."

Two days passed. The trappers crossed several long, open meadows which in summer would have provided a feast of forage; now there was none. Late in the day some pasture was found, but for several of the animals it was too late: "This evening it was again decided to kill three more of our horses."

It seemed to be the greatest cruelty to take your rifle, when your horse sinks to the ground from starvation, but still manifests a desire and willingness to follow you, to shoot him in the head and then cut him up & take such parts of their flesh as extreme hunger alone will render it possible for a human being to eat. This we done several times, and it was the only thing that saved us from death. 24 of our horses died since we arrived on top of the mountain—17 of which we eat the best parts.

Conditions worsened. Walker sent scouts in search of game and a clear route through the mountains, but they returned without finding either.

We were at a complete stand. No one was acquainted with the country, nor no person knew how wide the summit of this mountain was. —We had travelled for five days since we arrived at what was supposed to be the summit—were now still surrounded with snow and rugged peaks—the vigour of every man almost exhausted—nothing to give our poor horses, which were no longer any assistance to us in travelling, but a burthen, for we had to help the most of them along as we would an old and feeble man.

"Our situation was growing more distressing every hour," he added, "and all we now thought of, was to extricate ourselves from this inhospitable region."

A day of rare beauty unfolds around me. Sky and forest tremble with color; the scent of evergreen is torrid. All of Virginia Canyon holds not a patch of snow. At McCabe Creek I slip from my pack and lie contentedly in the sun, gorging myself on cheese and dried fruit.

Sated, I wander along the stream. It is beautiful here; I'm traveling a different planet from the one Zenas walked. He struggled a few miles through mountains of snow each day and gnawed like a wild animal on frozen horse meat at night. I would cover eighteen miles today, eat well, enjoy the scenery, and suffer only from loneliness.

I ask myself, How can I possibly see the Sierra as he did?

A log lies rotting beside the creek. I crawl onto it and run my fingers over its crumbling bark. The bark is rough and dusty, like paint chipping from an old fence; it flakes off at a touch.

The log was a tree that stood here straight and tall in 1833. It ruled this part of the forest. Suddenly I have an inkling of an answer to my question. Though the log crumbles into dust, it is as alive as ever. I feel it beneath me, huge and solid. Its muddy aroma delights me. Insects dash madly along it on their way to important affairs. Powdery debris floats softly to the ground. For me no less than for Leonard, this tree—indeed, this creek, this streamside, this deep wide canyon—is new and strange and alive. When he passed through the canyon was terra incognita; when I pass through it is terra incognita too, a land as wild and weird and mysterious as the far side of the moon, a land I have never seen.

I see no reason to place a premium on priority. The sight of a tree or a mountain can't be used up like a bar of soap; it's recyclable. Each view of this canyon today or a thousand years from today is a fresh look at the forest primeval. Each image that registers on my consciousness is a cameo to cherish. In this sparkling moment, a tree long dead takes root again in the moist and fertile soil of Virginia Canyon.

"I used to envy the father of our race, dwelling as he did in contact with the new-made fields and plants of Eden," wrote John Muir. "But I do so no more, because I have discovered that I also live in 'creation's dawn.' The morning stars still sing together, and the world, not yet half made, becomes more beautiful every day."

I shoulder my pack. The bittersweet scent of the lodgepole forest envelops me as I climb five hundred feet up the south wall of the canyon, traverse a ridgetop, then descend into the silver-green depths of Cold Canyon. The name is a joke. It is warm here. The forest closes in around me. The peaks disappear behind the treetops and I enter an intriguing world of deadfalls and dry streambeds, boulders great and small, crazy twists in the canyon, rises and dips, dry flowers dying, lightning-downed trees sliced lengthwise like French bread. I am bound for Glen Aulin, a popular destination for overnighters hiking in from the Tioga Road several hours ahead. Even in midweek a few campers should be there. It's of little importance to me that they be campers, however, as long as they are *talkers*. The miles pass effortlessly as I take in the fine sights and blithely discuss them aloud with myself.

Conditions at last began to improve for Walker and his men. They crossed the Tuolumne River not far from Glen Aulin, then continued toward the southwest, traveling along the divide between the Tuolumne and the Merced River. They made two extraordinary discoveries: some lofty precipices that appeared to be more than a mile high—almost certainly Yosemite Valley—and huge trees "16 to 18 fathoms around the trunk": sequoias. Before them a cheering vista of California's great central plain opened up. They shot both deer and bear, and ate them "in less time than a hungry wolf would devour a lamb." No animal larger than a rabbit had been taken since they left the Great Salt Lake; no meat other than horse flesh had been eaten in two weeks.

Crazy though he may have been, one foot and most of the other thrust voluntarily into his grave, Walker had succeeded in crossing—and taming—the wild Sierra. And because the first task after taming something is to give it a name, it wasn't long after that the mountain without a name was christened. On the return trip Leonard called it "the Calafornia mountain." Within a few years it became known everywhere as the Sierra Nevada, the Snowy Range.

A sigh of relief comes over Leonard's journal as he and his mates drop over the final ridge. None of the party had perished during the crossing from Willow Springs, a journey that had taken more than three weeks. Now just a few weeks ahead lay San Francisco Bay, and beyond that—

"Ocian in view. O! the joy!"

The words are William Clark's, written on his arrival at the mouth of the Columbia in 1805. In the literature of exploration his eloquence has surely never been surpassed. But the depth of his emotion may well have been equaled in 1833 when Joe and the boys came up on land's end, and gazed at last on the ocean of their dreams, the Pacific.

One final embellishment to round out the tale. Sometime in the early 1830s, word reached Leonard's parents that their son had been killed on his way west. Their grief can well be imagined, but it was not destined to last. For one day a few years later, Zenas Leonard, hickory knot, turned up at his parents' home in Clearfield, Pennsylvania. He was greeted as one returning from the dead. This happened in 1835, in the autumn.

On a bright and exciting October morning I wander down from Glen Aulin toward Yosemite Valley. Last night Glen Aulin was packed with campers. I spent the evening strolling from campfire to campfire, chattering like a mynah bird.

On a whim, I leave the trail and scramble up a slope that leads to a ridgetop. At the high point I'm greeted by a spectacular view. Spread out before me are the myriad scenes of yesterday—Cold Canyon and its deep forests in the foreground, tall gray peaks rising out of the trees, narrow streams winding toward the lowlands. In the distance, Virginia Canyon slopes up through the haze toward the shimmering crest of the Sierra.

And, covering it all, a surprise. While I slept last night, winter came to the high country. Now from the far horizon sweeping down almost to Glen Aulin, a soft and beautiful blanket of snow lies on the landscape.

I stand atop the ridge bewitched by the scene. It is many miles from here to my bus stop in the valley. But mountains are dead beneath the snow. I'll stand here, patient as the moon, and watch over the silent peaks till the breath of life returns.

Fourfold

Visions

of the Gila

Stick to Facts, sir!
CHARLES DICKENS, *Hard Times*

What am I doing saying "foxtail pine"?
GARY SNYDER, *"Foxtail Pine"*

I

These must be discouraging times for never-say-die rationalists who continue to insist, with Descartes, that all the phenomena of nature can be deduced "with the clarity of a mathematical demonstration." Departing from a scientific tradition that during the Middle Ages had seen clarity of mathematical demonstration all but vanish into a murky brew of black magic, philosophy, astrology, rumor, and gimcrack experimentation, Descartes in the seventeenth century reintroduced rationality to the study of nature, declaring that science is "certain, evident knowledge." "We reject all knowledge which is merely probable and judge that only those things should be believed which are perfectly known and about which there can be no doubts."

Gazing back from an age in which *perfect* is an adjective reserved for the occasional baseball game and perfection is diagnosed as a neurotic fantasy, we must pause to admire the wondrous optimism of so mad a plan. Descartes, of course, was anything but mad, but, like many a revolutionary, he was driven to an improvident excess by the stench of the status quo. Medieval science was undeniably malodorous, so he tossed it out, bubbling cauldron and all, and started from scratch. It happened that Descartes enjoyed using his head, always a revolutionary habit, so it was here that his revolution began. It is said that late one Sunday morning several of his friends burst in on him and were startled to find the sapient Frenchman still abed, seated bolt upright and staring intently into space.

"What are you doing?" they inquired.

"Thinking!" he cried. They were so appalled that they stormed out of the house, leaving him to sin in peace. In 1637 Descartes published his *Discourse on Method*, the ground-breaking treatise in which he argued that his favorite pastime was no mere diversion but in fact the key to perfect knowledge. True science must proceed from thought organized along logical lines. Doubt must become preeminent; truth must be tested in the light of its "clear and distinct intelligibility." Not many years before, Francis Bacon had begun touting the virtues of careful observation and the accumulation of facts to all who would understand nature. When Descartes's rationalism was added to Bacon's empiricism, black magic was out, the scientific method in. In fundamentally the same garb it remains with us to this day.

The results have been spectacular. The medieval serf rode to work in an ox-cart; his modern counterpart drives a fuel-injected Camaro. The alchemists of old searched unsuccessfully for the elixir of life; rational science discovered it—a low-cholesterol, high-fiber diet. That electric apple peelers, computer art, and plastic roses may seem scant improvements over their medieval equivalents is not an indictment of modern science, but proof of its bounteousness. By staying in bed on Sunday morning Descartes created something for everyone. The crank who rails at science and technology must be prepared to throw out his refrigerator along with his processed cheese.

How astonishing it is, then, that after three hundred and fifty years of viewing the universe in this monumentally different and profitable way, almost no one believes what he sees. It is not just latter-day astrologers and cauldron tenders who continue to perceive in nature the ghostly outlines of medieval magic and mystery; mainstream Americans see them too. In overwhelming numbers they persist in believing that there is something enchanted, something nonrational, out there; and, equally amazing, that watching over it and them and their Polaroid cameras from his home in the sky there is a supreme and unknowable God.

Nor are scientists themselves fully committed Cartesians. Einstein made frequent excursions into theology; Pascal contended that the heart has its reasons which reason does not know. In the literature of our day, departures from orthodoxy are common: Rachel Carson confessing that she could not write about the sea and leave out the poetry; Lewis Thomas succumbing to the wonder of the beavers and the otters in the Tucson Zoo. Such lapses should not surprise us, for scientists are trained observers, and what they observe in their research often clashes with some personal reality that they hold dear. More often than most of us, they confront the ambiguities that led Nabokov to remark that the word "reality" should never be used except in quotation marks.

Think, for example, of wildlife biologists who develop deep personal relationships with the animals they study. Because they cannot digitize their emotions they are unable to marshal them as data in their studies. Animals they know to be thinking, feeling creatures they are forced to portray in Baconian monographs as mindless automatons (incidentally, the conclusion about nonhumans reached by Descartes).

Or again: Neurologists and researchers into artificial intelligence brilliantly tame the lawless mind, demonstrating that our grocery lists and vacation plans are nothing more than electrical zings and zaps, simple cause-and-effect, really, ordered by codes and algorithms. Yet before the taunting specters of art, intuition, creativity, love, and a thousand other nonelectrical phenomena, these same men and women stand mute and helpless and sometimes awed.

Or again: Astronomers discover the secret of the universe, a catastrophic undoing which in a fraction of a second yielded up the cosmic flotsam from which we have fashioned everything from the Parthenon to pinball machines. Yet when the sun has set and a soft wind stirs among the linden leaves, our sage Cartesians steal out into the mystical moist night air, and there, with Whitman, look up in perfect silence at the stars.

Even single-vision scientists, their eyes glued firmly to the gauges of their instruments, are finding it harder and harder to believe what they see. The anomalies began to appear in the 1920s when quantum physicists discovered that, in defiance of Bacon, certain measurements they sought were, quite simply, unattainable. They could measure an atomic particle's position or they could measure its momentum, but they could never measure both. It wasn't the fault of their measuring devices; an *absolute* barrier to such knowledge existed. Put more brutally: there are some things we can never know.

With this discovery a rather exotic humility began to creep into the more scrupulous scientific laboratories. It spread quickly when Cartesian self-assurance suffered a second and equally humbling blow. First in atomic physics, then in other disciplines it became apparent that the notion of an objective observer measuring remote nature—a central assumption of the scientific method—was flawed.

The reasons were many and complex, but they were summed up nicely by E. B. White when an admirer of his nature essays asked him if he watched birds. "Yes," replied White, "and they watch me." Science had uncovered a previously unsuspected continuum between observer and observed; the experimenter, it seemed, was doomed to participate in his own experiment. The scientist who set out dispassionately to measure nature measured a nature altered by his measurements. "What we observe," wrote Werner Heisenberg, one of the chief instigators of this depressing business, "is not nature itself, but nature exposed to our method of questioning." Quite unexpectedly, to rationalists at least, the universe turned out to have a maddening ebb and flow that prevented them from getting their hands on any part of it with complete assurance. While they prepared to pounce on an explanation for one phenomenon, another slithered out of sight like a wily trout; if they managed somehow to corner number two, number one vanished. Almost overnight the hope of pure Cartesian truth was dashed.

Not everyone was surprised. Many not ordained to the ministry of science had understood the limitations of rationalism long before Heisenberg happened along. Hear the words spoken in 1852 by the Duwamish chief Sealth, a man who had never studied atomic physics: "All things are connected like the blood that unites us all. Man did not weave the web of life, he is merely a strand in it. Whatever he does to the web, he does to himself."

Needless to say, the words of this sagacious American Indian were disregarded, and even those of Heisenberg have been slow to gain acceptance. Lowering the scientist into his own petri dish introduced the inconvenience of responsibility to the operations of science, and many have found it more expedient to remain faithful to the anachronistic conceit of detached observation. Yet the tenor is clear: no behavioral psychologist can blindly dismiss the effect he has on his rats as he marches them through their paces; no chemist can relinquish responsibility for the uses to which his potions are put. Ducking accountability, Sealth and Heisenberg would agree, is bad medicine and bad science.

Naturally, a few scientists are getting edgy. In the spring of 1988, experiments by a highly respected French researcher seemed to confirm the claims of homeopathists previously dismissed as quacks. Results obtained by Jacques Benveniste and his team at INSERM, the French equivalent of the U.S. National Institutes of Health, established that a "resonant" effect in water molecules allowed the molecules to "remember" a substance no longer in solution. French water seemed to have a brain. The august British science journal *Nature* reluctantly published the results, but not without labeling them, in an editorial, "unbelievable." Then in an unprecedented operation undertaken to expose what they were certain was bare and shameless fraud, *Nature's* editors dispatched a team of debunkers to Paris, where they invaded Benveniste's lab, diddled his test tubes, and rifled his books, all in the name of True and Perfect Science.

They failed. But of course: in related tests, Seymour Antelman at the University of Pittsburgh was getting precisely the same results. Black magic was back! Just in case there were any lingering doubts, researchers at the Harvard School of Public Health reported at almost the same time a result as unbelievable as Benveniste's: certain bacteria seemed to be able to control the way they mutated. Evolutionary biology posits random mutations; Harvard's bacteria mutated in a manner that was "directed." Who or what was directing them no one on the research team was willing to guess. But in their paper announcing the results, John Cairns and his colleagues gushed rather unscientifically: "Now almost anything seems possible."

For three hundred and fifty years scientists had painstakingly carved the universe into smaller and smaller parts, confident that an understanding of the parts would lead to an understanding of the whole. Yet, as Fritjof Capra has so brilliantly documented in *The Turning Point*, the effort has been a failure. Much has been learned about the mechanics of the universe, but the goal of understanding it, of discovering some ultimate truth or reality, has never been achieved. Had Descartes been wrong? That hardly seemed possible. The achievements of the revolution he fathered have been undeniably wondrous. Might we, then, be on the threshold of yet another revolution, one that might take the best of the last and combine it with something new, and perhaps something old, in a renewed and even more powerful assault on the nature of "reality"?

II

For nearly a week warm rains had pounded the high desert, swamping the arroyos and reducing the bright vermilion mesas to an unsightly shaggy-dog brown. In the rest of the nation it was the first year of the Great Drought, but New Mexico, as usual, had not been notified. Several times a day Carol and I tuned in to the local weathercasts for news of clearing. At last it came: the lunatic front was moving on; in the western portion of the state clear skies were forecast for the next several days. By midmorning we were packed and on the road, speeding south and west toward the storied outback, the mountain wilderness that New Mexicans call the Gila.

I know of no place where the contrast between nebulous nature and premium unleaded science is more vivid, or more consequential, than it is in New Mexico. For every ghostly mountain peak and tumbleweed-haunted upland there is a physicist or electrical engineer—more Ph.D.s here per capita than in any other state. In 1930 a beardless prophet named Robert Goddard wandered onto New Mexico's biblical eastern plains, as inscrutable a landscape as you are likely to find. There, with liquid-fuel rockets that he jerry-rigged from scrap metal and sweet-talked into the heavens, he personally invented the Space Age. Within a decade brawny missiles the size of alfalfa silos were lifting off from White Sands, a shimmering phantasm of shifting gypsum dunes. Farther north, in the balmy valley of the Rio Grande and on a verdant mesa overlooking it, the Sandia and Los Alamos National Laboratories sprang up. Now the state's second and third largest employers (the Albuquerque school system is first), the two put scientists to work by the thousands fashioning ever more sophisticated technologies, mostly for military purposes.

The schizophrenic vistas that result from this bewildering chiasma provide interesting tests of the body's ability to absorb irony. It is usually argued that we moderns have so swiftly succumbed to technology that we have not yet evolved a means for dealing with its more baroque side effects. But I think we have. The family dog has evolved the same means for dealing with the tension of conflicting drives—say, the choice between a juicy soup bone and a frolic in the park. Animal behaviorists call it displacement. Confronted with rockets in the desert, we neither laugh nor cry nor defiantly choose one over the other; instead we plunk down on our haunches and begin vigorously scratching our heads. In the sweet morning haze embracing the pines of the Pajarito Plateau float aboriginal incantations. Listen: Cochiti Indians are chanting, scattering cornmeal to the stone lions in gratitude for a successful hunt. Beyond rise the labs of Los Alamos, solemn and slate-gray, bound in chainlink fences and warning signs. I visited once, expecting to stay the night. Moments after driving into town I was mysteriously overcome by symptoms commonly associated with the consumption of tainted shellfish. My head swam, my stomach boiled. Unable to handle the physics of Los Alamos, I was on my way—and cured—within minutes.

Or consider a rudimentary expanse of grasslands lying just north of the Gila, an extinct Pleistocene lakebed called the Plains of San Agustin. It is so long and so wide and so unabashed that some say it outdistances the sky. Speeding across the plains toward a crossroads called Datil, a name no one can explain, a driver suddenly begins to hallucinate. In the frantic emptiness there are no reference points. Motion ceases; the earth melts away. The car is snatched up by the tentacles of infinity. The wheels spin in the fathomless blue.

Then, ahead, at first mere specks in the void, growing larger and larger as earth is regained and time and motion resume and accelerate, not buffalo or pronghorn or an Apache war party, somehow the first possibilities that enter the mind, but radio dishes! radio dishes! dozens of them, each looking as large as Rhode Island. Here from the ashes of the Pleistocene has risen the Very Large Array, the largest radio telescope in the world (actually twenty-seven interconnecting antennae)—its purpose, gossip with the cosmos. Think of lox and mosquito repellant. Think of measles and croquet. Think of Keats and a Big Mac. If you can process these nerve-shattering miscegenations, perhaps you are cut out to probe the endless skies near Datil for news from the stars. Perhaps you are cut out for New Mexico.

Of course, the most nerve-shattering miscegenation of them all now lies just thirty miles from us as we sink back under the numbing hum of pistons and stare down the interstate south of Socorro. Carol has the wheel. I scrunch down further in my seat and turn to survey the horizon to the east—above San Antonio and the World's Finest Green Chili Cheeseburger and Bosque del Apache, where on a winter's night you can welcome home the whooping cranes, giddy from the flight, from the wonderment that one more once-forbidden season lies tucked safely beneath their wings.

"There," I say. Somehow the word catches in my throat. I gesture toward Oscura Peak, the mountain that was witness, now faint beneath a desert haze that roils like incense. And for a moment we pretend to imagine the quiet dawn, the deft plunge from the tower, the moment that escaped from time, the brightness of a thousand suns that caused Oppenheimer to go irrational, to invoke the Bhagavad-Gita—to scratch his magnificent head. That gave a name to this place: Trinity Site.

It is called the Land of Enchantment, but perhaps New Mexico should be known as the Land of Ages. The Space Age, the Nuclear Age, the Age When We Reached for the Stars—all of these hallowed spans began here. Lest we forget the ghostly mountains, the aboriginal incantations, let us crown a different kind of age that also breathed first in

New Mexico, a counterpoise to telescopes and thermonuclear devices. Some might call it the Age of Preservation; I prefer to call it the Age of Reenchantment. Not far from Taos yawns a rude gorge of inchoate terror, ripped from the high tableland, it might appear, by the claw of a passing pterodactyl. Through this rent in the earth's skin pours the young and impetuous Rio Grande—not the meek and meandering river-to-be, but a black, caterwauling, diamond-tossing demon of a river, so mad that in 1968 it was designated one of the nation's first eight Wild and Scenic Rivers. A stab at saving the earth.

Ahead of us now, a deep shadow on the blue horizon, sprawls the rolling Gila, where in 1924 a christening of even greater importance took place. Three years earlier, at the conclusion of an article in the *Journal of Forestry*, the indispensable Aldo Leopold recommended that part of the Gila National Forest be set aside as a wilderness preserve, permanently protected from development. It should be "big enough to absorb a two weeks' pack trip," said Leopold, "devoid of roads, artificial trails, cottages, or other works of man."

That such an idea could have occurred to a young white American male is remarkable; that Leopold was at the time an employee of the U.S. Forest Service, an agency famous for its affection for downed timber, is occasion for a champagne toast. Leopold might have expected to be executed for heresy had he not found an ally in the Forest Service: landscape architect Arthur Carhart, an unsung hero of the preservation movement. Carhart and Leopold pressed their case, and in 1924 Frank Pooler, chief forester for the region, did the unthinkable: he set aside 574,000 acres of the Gila as officially protected "wilderness," the first such designation of more than a few acres ever made anywhere in the world. Banned forever from the Gila were roads, logging, motorized vehicles, vacation homes, golf courses, tennis courts, souvenir stores, Santa Claus villages, and hamburger stands. What Pooler did was worse than unthinkable: it was a demanifestation of destiny.

Had it been possible to view the earth from space that watershed year, it might have appeared to some inquiring extraterrestrial that, just in the nick of time, earthlings had found a cure for the deadly asphalt virus that had threatened to destroy their planet. Spreading ever faster across the globe's land masses, the pernicious gray tendrils had suddenly come up against an island of indomitable green in the American Southwest and had inexplicably been stopped cold.

Thus the Gila, Ground Zero in the Age of Reenchantment. Broadly speaking it comprises three parts. To the east lies the Black Range, a vast backland of ridge-and-canyon corduroy still running on primordial standard time. I first saw the range from a distant pass in a light rain. Shrouded in mist, it took on the compelling quality of myth. Clearly visible was that primitive aspect of nature famous for repelling the righteous, so gladly does it tingle in their loins. A confession: These tingles do not repel me. Nay and verily, my loins seek them out. My recommendation to all, especially the righteous, is a romp in the Black Range.

In the west the pink desert hangs out of Arizona like a parched tongue. It laps feebly against the sharp upthrust of New Mexico's Mogollon Mountains and dries up. Here burnt-amber walls and bald summits tower nearly six thousand feet above the surrounding plains. The heart of the Gila lies between the two regions and, like both of them, it startles the first-time visitor expecting a drop-dead wasteland of sage and jackrabbit. Both are here on the edges, but they are not the Gila. The Gila is a surprising country of cool rivers winding through red-rock canyons, of steep mountains bucking under forests of aspen, spruce, and fir, and of playgrounds for elk, black bear, deer, and antelope.

But consider the catch, the Great November Loophole. Play here if you wish, deer and antelope, but if it is November and you want to be preserved incarnate in this wilderness preserve, be vigilant, or you may be preserved, dry-lipped and glassy-eyed, watching over someone's martini shaker in Terre Haute, Indiana. For in November the sportsmen come sporting, and the Gila rises up to proclaim one of its several disagreements with the tenets of the Age of Preservation—as indeed do all of the units in the nation's wilderness preservation system, a system which upon inspection reveals itself as only selectively preservationist. It preserves trees but not mammals (hunting is allowed in wilderness areas). It preserves flowers but not fish (fishing is allowed). It preserves insects but not grass (grazing is allowed). It preserves soils but not minerals (mining of claims established before 1985 is allowed). The nation's wilderness preservation system preserves good intentions but not mammals, fish, grass, or minerals. Does such a system preserve wilderness? Imagine a museum that preserves van Goghs, all but the yellows and the blues. Does it preserve van Goghs?

Of the four notable shortcomings in the wilderness preservation system, the system's failure to preserve mammals rankles me most. I used to think that my curious views on hunting were rooted in the equally curious refusal of my father to teach me how to shoot out a deer's eyes. But I recently met a man whose father did not refuse, a man who under his father's patient tutelage learned to shoot out a deer's eyes with marvelous adroitness, severing the optic nerve but leaving intact the iris; but who on a mysteriously clear morning in the November of his twenty-third year gazed long enough through his rifle sights to *see*— and never pulled the trigger again. I wish I knew what expanded that man's vision; I know only that it wasn't rationalism. Rationalism is too plodding. For all of its virtues, it can never be startled, for it is unable to leap. Thus it gives us a hunt that is stupefied sporting after game instead of the sacred mission it once was, when the sport was ritual, when the game were fellow creatures revered and respected, when the hunter lay down with his prey face to face and took in the final breath and thanked the animal for the precious gift of its life spirit. "Those who were sacred have remained so," Denise Levertov reminds us in "Come into Animal Presence":

> holiness does not dissolve, it is a presence
> of bronze, only the sight that saw it
> faltered and turned from it.

The sight faltered. This disturbs me greatly. Descartes began by thinking. What are we to think of thinking? Ludwig Wittgenstein probed longer and harder into the nature of thought than I shall ever be capable of doing, and was distressed enough at what he found to shout: "Don't think: Look!" I am encouraged by his results. Wittgenstein's thoughtful words I have adopted as my motto for November.

Scientists have thought enough about the Gila to have solved many of its mysteries, though not all. Safe, sanitized, and value-free, the results of scientific research are passed on to the visitor in the form of "information," the dread I-word, rationalism's most embarrassing creation. "Be joyful though you have considered all the facts," counsels the ever-patient Wendell Berry, but the tyranny of information conspires mightily against joy. How are we to emerge joyfully from a reading of the following teeth-gnashers, taken from the official map of the Gila National Forest prepared for visitors by the U.S. Forest Service?

Under "Forage": "Cattle mean meat and leather for America and a living for many ranchers."

Under "Timber": "On the cool, green mountains of the Gila National Forest are 400,000 acres of commercial forest with nearly 1.7 billion board feet of standing sawtimber. About 80 percent of the commercial trees are ponderosa pine, limber pine, and Englemann spruce. Each year the Gila sawlog harvest brings about a quarter of a million dollars to the Federal treasury."

Under "Water": "Downstream, particularly on the Gila River, the water that runs off the mountains is highly valued for domestic, industrial, agricultural, and recreational uses."

And here, an extended section on "Wildlife":

Wildlife and fish are other valuable resources of the Gila National Forest. Each year thousands of hunters flock to the forest in search of sport. They play a part in keeping the number of game animals in balance with their food supply. The sportsmen are also an important source of income for the merchants of nearby communities.

The most numerous big game species on the Gila is the Rocky Mountain mule deer. There are several thousand of the beautiful Sonoran whitetailed deer. Elk have been reintroduced into the high country and provide excellent hunting. Antelope find forage on some of the grasslands, and black bear are found in the timbered elevations. A few javelina, or wild pig, live in the warmer parts of the Gila, but no open season has been held in recent years. In 1964 bighorn sheep were reintroduced into the Gila country and eventually may be plentiful enough to hunt.

That is all we learn of the elk, the sheep, and the pig, which a visitor from another planet might be forgiven for confusing with the clay pigeon. When the eyes of the deer have been shot out, when trees are a cash crop, when cattle mean meat and leather for America, our view of the Gila slouches dangerously toward blindness. Only a dim shadow remains, the rigid and unreassuring outlines of our old friend information.

What is saddest about the situation is that no one truly wants it that way. No one—no hunter, no angler, no tourist, no manager, no forest ranger, no logger, no hiker, no scientist—no one truly views the Gila as information. We come, one and all, because of a fire that burns within us, a deep yearning to touch the earth as our ancestors did and feel the pulse of life within—*if only the rules allowed*. A famous memo from the director of the U.S. Army Corps of Engineers suggests how far we have to go:

Subject: Improper Terminology
I am observing a growing trend in the use of the verb "to feel." Please avoid its use in any paper that you may prepare for my signature. Any action that I take is supposed to be objective, emotionally sterile, and totally devoid of all feeling . . . please see that your work is purged of this offensive word.

What fevers, what lonely nights gave rise to these ravings I leave to others to search out. Let me only suggest that such self-imposed impoverishment of expression is a means of self-mutilation. We might as well blind ourselves with lasers or rip out our vocal cords as sign on with the engineers. The damage to our sight has been great, but a glimmer remains. Here in the mountains of New Mexico we seek a bold new metascience, one capable of restoring our own sight and that of the brown-eyed deer.

The flats become foothills; the road narrows to two lanes. After a week of rain the lustrous countryside is smiling bashfully, shaking itself like a poodle after a bath. Here and there we come upon a crossroads with a name, its general store and filling station deployed so casually side by side that it seems they might switch places in the morning. These happy-go-lucky carstops inspire you with their timberline resilience. They remind me of the spiders I once found at twelve thousand feet, smack in the middle of a huge Sierra snowfield—miles from greenery, light years from prudence, jitterbugging happily because snowfields, by God, are what happened, and anyway we like it here.

The historical markers beside the road tell of Billy the Kid, of silver-time boom-and-bust, of Butch Cassidy and his Wild Bunch, and the Apaches Victorio and Goyathlay, the one they called Geronimo. Alas, more information. The epic tale of Geronimo is reduced to a sorry litany of dragnets and APBs. Something is missing: How was it that this Apache shaman eluded capture year after year? What did he read in the lupine and the larkspur that we do not? Why did he return again and again to the hot pools of the Gila—was it simply pleasure or was there more to it than that? We yearn for stories like the ones that Geronimo himself told of his childhood in the country surrounding the headwaters of the Gila River: "I was warmed by the sun, rocked by the winds, and sheltered by the trees as other Indian babes. When a child my mother taught me the legends of our people; taught me of the sun and sky, the moon and stars, the clouds and storms." In the cadences of this wind-rocked fugitive, in the rhythm of words that toss with the rolling earth, we hear for the first time the unspoiled heartsong of the Gila.

Forty miles from Silver City the road, now a serpentine mountain lane, winds to an end at Gila Cliff Dwellings National Monument—40 RMS RVR VU, a mystery science is powerless to explain. Two hundred years before Columbus stepped ashore on Watling Island, members of a culture known as the Mogollon inhabited these airy caves on the west fork of the Gila River, enjoying superb protection in a garden spot of unsurpassed beauty. Mysteriously, they disappeared without a trace.

Not many make it here today. On a placid spring morning you can follow the swallows high up into a lush canyon silhouetted in ponderosa, and there, alone, don the robes of the vanished race that is you. The smoke-blackened ceilings tell of community feasts and singalongs, of magical nights when Grandfather blew your mind with the stories of Coyote's Revenge and the Skeleton Who Lived by the Beanfield. The dust lies fresh on the windowsills. The view under the grand arch is as familiar as yesterday. A featherlight haze hangs in the canyon before you. As the sun lifts higher, the veil draws back and the air lights up with lacewings and dragonflies.

"The women averaged 5 feet, 1 inch and the men about 5 feet, 5 inches in height. They were slight of build, yet muscular." The National Park Service brochure languishes in my hands like an unwanted sandwich. "They had dark hair and eyes and brown skin. The men wore headbands."

My eyes glaze over. I recall a visit to the magnificent cliff dwellings at Mesa Verde, and the powerlessness I felt there trying to understand another vanished race through appeal to the "evidence"—the shards and headbands, the fragments left behind. Is a man his hunting spear, a woman her earthenware bowl? Am I my socket-wrench set? Like the dutiful anthropologist I rummaged through garbage in search of "them," forgetting that I was part of the experiment. Mesa Verde was cold, dead rock until I pulled my nose from my guidebook and joined hands with its people—singing and dancing with them, breathing their pure air, marveling with them at hawks and violets, reviving in their cool canyon breeze. Mesa Verde came alive when I admitted its reenchantment.

"How did they ever get down there?" I had wondered aloud, unsatisfied with the official explanation that had residents clambering down to their aeries by means of shallow steps carved into frightfully steep rock. What about the old folks? What about days it rained or snowed?

"Maybe they flew," said Carol, and I knew at once that she was right.

The Mogollon arrived in the Gila valley around A.D. 100 and remained for more than a thousand years. During most of their stay they inhabited conventional dwellings, moving into their sky homes only during the final thirty or forty years. The Mogollon abandoned the cliffs and departed the region sometime in the early 1300s. Science strikes out: "Why they left and where they went are not known." With that the writer is freed and his brochure can at last reach for the truth: "For generations, the sounds of their voices and laughter echoed in the canyons. And then there were only the sounds of the streams and birds."

It is the beginning of poetry, another clue to unlocking the unsolved mysteries of the Gila.

The trail lights out across a weathered tableland dotted with juniper and pine. Footloose at last, we two-step under blue satin skies till, half an hour out, we stumble upon a somber stand of cowboys glowering down at us from saddle height. Red-eyed and tongue-tied, they are deep in a communal flask of the devil's brew.

This land is their land. We warble two-fisted howdies and hurry on. Ten minutes later we flush out a pair of teenaged boys leading their horses upcountry. The boys are outfitted in chaps and ten-gallon hats; one brandishes a .44 Magnum handgun that burns hot as the latest *Hustler* in his hands.

A moment of panic sparks up my spine. Guns do that to me. I once had a Saturday Night Special pressed to my temple by a member of a gang of teenagers in New York City. While the gunman shouted instructions, several of his cohorts jabbed switchblades into various of my parts while several others explored me for booty. I survived that gun and I survived this one, but I still don't like the things.

Where the trail joins the middle fork of the Gila River we turn west, and now and for the next three days blend our lives with that of the river. The blending is one in fact, for so narrow is the canyon, so relentless its thousand-foot walls, that for much of the way the trail must escape into the Gila itself. Every few minutes we leave the shade of riverside cottonwoods and plunge knee-deep into the water, walking sticks poled hard against the current. Our acclimatization to this curious life is swift: it is merely a matter of remembering. The first meeting with the waters is cold and awkward, a true breaking of the ice; before long we are slipping in like salamanders.

These dwellers of the cliffs, then—who exactly were they? On the mountain named Nulus, Pliny reports, there are people with their feet turned backwards and with eight toes on each foot, while on many of the mountains live tribes of human beings with dogs' heads, who wear coverings of wild beasts' skins, whose speech is a bark, and who live by hunting and fowling, for which they use their nails as weapons. The Machlyes perform the function of either sex alternately. The Triballi and the Illyrians have two pupils in each eye; they bewitch at a glance and kill those they stare at for a longer time.

Somewhere we encounter a band of five young German men clad in the briefest of attire. After several weeks of schmoozing in the Southwest they have evolved skin red as the canyon walls. Today they are trotting upstream toting plastic air mattresses under their arms. They should be driving BMWs but they have discovered something even better: hypertravel on the Gila. At the launch site they pause for the thrill, then leap into the water like drunken frogs. A moment later they join the current and, waving happily, sail off in their pea-green boats.

When we are not with the river we are with the alder, the willow, and the wild grape. Underfoot the earth is sand or cobblestone, a few yards to our right or left thirty-million-year-old rhyolite, andesite, and tuff.

Once, on a ramble with Ralph Waldo Emerson, the clear-eyed Transcendentalist Margaret Fuller rambled smack into a tree.

"Didn't you see that tree?" asked her startled companion.

"I saw it," replied Fuller. "I just didn't *realize* it."

Profusions of golden columbine tumble at us from bushes beside the trail. Someone once asked Edward Abbey to identify an unfamiliar desert plant. Abbey gazed at the plant for a moment, then answered: "What it *is*, no one knows. But men call it creosote bush. *Larrea tridentata*."

In the late afternoon we make camp in an open grove of ponderosa forty yards from the river. Our fellow lodgers are baffling fellows we come to call pepper bugs. They are the size of large molecules, too small to notice until a streak the color of cayenne pepper appears mysteriously on a finger or shirt sleeve, the record of an inadvertent squish. Streaks appear by the dozens. Like photons in a bubble chamber, these creatures are known only by their passing. I strain my eyes at a live one setting out across my sneaker with all the pluck and majesty of Chichester riding full on the evening tide. Squinting hard, I attempt to count the number of oars this fellow swings. Is it six or eight? Is it insect or spider? What is the point of pepper bugs? Why does the river chatter?

A wondrous discovery: fifty feet up the cliffside a rockbound warm pool, fed by a trickling stream. The grotto is hidden by the trees, bound in a dense tangle of greenery. The water is hip-deep, warm and gentle as mint tea.

Explain this sleepy lagoon. Explain the fragrance of the leaves. Explain the whisper of the wind. Explain Geronimo. Explain how he disappeared. Did he come to this warm pool? If so, did he come in his own form or in that of a coyote? If he came, why did he come, and what did he read in the lupine and the larkspur? And why isn't the temperature of the water a million degrees more or less . . . why is it exactly the temperature of *me*?

There is room in the pool for twenty, but for a morning we have the waters to ourselves, with a seat by the eastern wall. Suspended between heaven and earth, we lie back, close our eyes, listen to the thunder of spreading circles when one of us accidentally moves a toe. We are Geronimo of the deep willows. We are the dark-haired dwellers of the cliffs. In the afternoon John and Debbie, blithe wanderers from El Paso, slip off their togs and slide in beside us. It is not an intrusion; people belong together in the wilderness. From the trailhead the two have thoughtfully packed in an enormous jug of refreshment, part Kool-Aid and part pure alcohol.

Men call it Wham-Bam. But what it *is*, no one knows.

III

I wanted to be a scientist. When I was fifteen or so someone gave me a Christmas present that almost overnight transformed me from shiftless teenager to young man with a mission. The gift was a handheld optical device, something like a slide viewer, that could be loaded with miniature illuminated star maps. By peering into the viewer with one eye while gazing at the night sky with the other, the observer played a wonderful trick of superimposition on the brain: the old confusing heavens suddenly appeared laid out neatly with dotted lines delineating the constellations and labels assigning the stars their proper names. The effect recalled a nature trail in a city park with its trees and flowers conveniently identified on plastic tags—except that this nature trail was light years away.

I read the instructions on the box with a mounting sense of excitement. Here at last was a guide to a world I had always wanted to visit. When darkness fell I bundled up, strapped on my rubber boots, and tramped out into the deep snow in my backyard. That night I fell in love with the heavens.

In the months to come I spent countless hours alone in the frozen darkness behind my house. It is not correct to say "behind my house," I suppose, for from the moment I slipped a map into the viewer and held it to my eye I was always in another place, propelled there by that timeless affection for the cosmos that inhabits us all, if only we allow

ourselves to remember. I came to know the bears, the twins, Andromeda and her silver-blue cloud, the soft light from which had set out two
million years before, and now, after surviving many a peril, had drifted
to rest in my eyes. The night sky changed from the dimensionless jumble of twinkles I had glanced up at unfeelingly from time to time to a
profound wonderment that cast a personal, obsessing spell over me. I
began to believe that if I tried hard I might be taken into the confidence
of the stars.

I read everything I could about astronomy. I devoured every book in
the public library's collection, and when I had read them all I started
over again. I learned of forces and energies, of the spin of galaxies, of
sumptuous heat and cold. Each evening in my backyard I turned my
face to the sky. Soon a year had passed, and Orion had wheeled round
again, and I had seen it all. My mind was made up: I would be an astronomer.

In April of my senior year in high school I learned that I had been
accepted into a special program of independent study in astronomy at
Harvard. Naturally, I was overjoyed. At the same time I was terrified of
Harvard's reputation for sophistication and arrogance and overpower-
ing difficulty. I was a skinny kid from a small town. I liked milk shakes
and Fats Domino. I didn't know if I was the right guy for the job.
Through the summer my apprehension grew, but as the day for my
departure drew near I began to take comfort in the knowledge that even
in cosmopolitan Cambridge I would be among friends. The stars of
Pennsylvania were the stars of Massachusetts too. We all travel the
same night sky.

A few days after my arrival in Cambridge I was given the keys to Harvard's venerable 15-inch refractor, now a bit creaky and dusty, but a
century before the largest refractor in the world. I shook my head in
disbelief. I had never gazed through a telescope. I'd dreamed of intimacy with Andromeda but had always imagined she was unattainable.
Now suddenly I had been handed the keys to her apartment!

Alas, we barely met. The beginning of science meant the end of intimacy. Across imponderable space the light of the silver stars had al-

ways traveled straight to my eyes (let us overlook the curiosities of relativity here). Now several obscuring barriers were thrown up at once. There was the telescope, of course; onto that I snapped a camera and into that I slipped film. For the next six months I sat at the controls of the telescope, not gazing at the sky, but photographing it. By the time I saw the stars they were white splotches on a sheet of emulsion. The white splotches, I learned in class, were rotating nuclear reactions converting hydrogen to helium.

I grew more and more depressed. The magic trick had been explained, had been robbed of its mystery. The poetry was gone; the wonder had sprouted wavelengths. I grew to dread my nights at the observatory. I didn't want to photograph the stars. I wanted to traipse out into the snow and gaze at them. The flaw in Cartesian reductionism had been exposed: analysis into smaller and smaller parts no more explained the cosmos than clusters of black notes on paper explained Bach. The whole is neither equal to nor greater than the sum of its parts. The whole has nothing to do with its parts!

I saw no reason to continue the charade. Investigation of a narrowly defined reality held no interest for me. Disillusioned, inordinately shy, I retreated into a world with no reality at all, one proud to proclaim its utter uselessness. In the spring I switched my major to mathematics.

"Out go sight, sound, taste, touch and smell," R. D. Laing has written of the sacrifices offered up by science in its quest for the grand elucidation—to which he quickly adds aesthetics, ethical sensibility, values, quality, form, feelings, motives, intentions, soul, and, as if more were needed, consciousness and spirit. For those to whom any of these may register as important or even as suspected elements of the truth, they are fatal sacrifices. Thus it is that the poets have relentlessly condemned Cartesian rationalism. For Poe, "science tore the summer dream beneath the tamarind tree." Goethe, Wordsworth, Whitman, Rilke, Rimbaud; Blake, the angriest of all:

> Now I a fourfold vision see
> And a fourfold vision is given to me

> Tis fourfold in my supreme delight
> And threefold in soft Beulahs night
> And twofold Always. May God us keep
> From Single vision & Newtons sleep

No one realizes the limitations of the Cartesian world view more fully than do scientists themselves when forced to choose between the objectifications of their professions and what they feel in their bones. Not long before his death I met a man who made that choice. Carl Koford was a wildlife biologist at the University of California at Berkeley. During a long and distinguished career, Koford had studied a whole arkload of species throughout the world in their native habitats. One of the animals he felt closest to was the California condor, a gravely endangered species that he had studied in the wild for three years and knew better than anyone alive. Koford fought valiantly, and ultimately unsuccessfully, against a proposal by the Audubon Society and the U.S. Fish and Wildlife Service to capture the few remaining wild condors in order to breed them in captivity. Unlike the public relations experts who ultimately prevailed, Koford had made the fatal mistake of coming to know the birds as more than mere flesh and blood. He fretted over the psychological pain that condors would suffer during capture and captivity. He argued that while genes and cells can surely be preserved in test tubes, the view of condors as genes and cells is woefully simplistic. What of a condor's *wildness?* he asked. That important part of what it is to be a condor cannot be preserved in captivity. Nor can what Koford characterized as "the complex cultural heritage" that animals in their native habitats pass from one generation to the next.

Descartes would probably agree. The consummate rationalist never argued that reductionism would yield the whole truth, merely that the truths it yielded were the only ones worth having. This bias came to define what it meant to *know*. To know something meant to reach it through logic. An oppressive prejudice arose. Knowledge became rational knowledge. To know a crocus or a maple was to know its biology. Any other kind of knowledge was fraudulent, and the means through which it was reached was labeled derisively as pseudoscience. Now, sensible people who wish to broaden their understanding of the world will not sully their hands with pseudoscience. Cloaking itself in the stifling authority of science, this misguided cousin turns a scientific eye on trans-scientific phenomena, with predictably laughable results. Thus logic is brought to bear on the occult, the psychic, the spiritual—legitimate and important areas of inquiry, but ones which in this manifold universe are not about to yield their secrets to rationality. We can no more find God through logic than we can find thermodynamics through meditation.

A determined assault on the truth must employ a variety of means, from science with its unparalleled ability to describe the machinery of nature, to Zen with its confidence that no description at all is needed, that it is better to see the face than to hear its name. Between the two lie a thousand different chemistries—art and myth, humor and magic, beauty, music, wonder, spirit, soul, and, what is often easiest to overlook, total and delighted bafflement. Such an assault promises us a grand synthesis of understanding, one which, I believe, will locate a place for us all in the cosmos, a glad sense that we are indeed part of the experiment, a kind of knowing that seeks not the account of an actual happening, as Borges wrote of poetry, but the expression of a longing.

IV

What might such a synthesis look like? Perhaps like the following, an assault on the truth as it might appear in a science book of the future (perhaps it will be called a reality book). We are all in this experiment together, we who have come to the Gila to savor its pleasures and inquire into its mysteries; our laboratory, a clearing in the forest deep in the wilds of New Mexico.

A peaceful evening has descended on the valley of the middle fork, slipping in almost imperceptibly behind a long and exhausting day of cloud-watching, rock-skipping, and steeping in the grotto by the columbines. We have shared a hearty supper during which we compared notes on the day's events and discussed our preliminary conclusions. Now the campfire crackles lustily, the night deepens, the dark ponderosas focus our vision on the newly sprouted stars. An owl sounds in the treetops above us; a coyote cries on a distant ridge. In the darkness the river lilts and tumbles. Here now a pot of tea—a spot of brandy, if you prefer. Breathe in the night, lean back to the rough-hewn log, stretch out in the soft duff. Who are we now (enter this in your notes)? Swift runners after antelope? Cave painters of Lascaux?

In the first moments of silence a flurry of thoughts light up the night like fireflies. But soon we abandon ourselves to the flames. Burning brighter, the fire takes command by circling round and drawing us in. Our thoughts resign authority; our vision blossoms forth. The transformation is accomplished: we feel a presence and turn to see that the animals have arrived.

In truth, at first we are uncertain, for the two are without depth or substance, mere shadows on the shapeless rock. We wait half-unbelieving (strangely, we are not afraid), and then in welcome one of us calls out. His shrill cry echoes off the cloistering walls, spirals down the tiled corridors of the canyon. When the last strain spins away, a fragile stillness settles in around us. We stare intently into the night, wondering if we are mistaken.

Then suddenly we sense movement. Miraculously, the shadows rise up out of the rocks. In steps as soft as eiderdown they traverse the void between us and emerge unformed into the firelight, where they blend for an instant with the dizzying shimmer of the flames; then they materialize . . . a wolf and a bear, fur and flesh, as real as jumbo jets. With the self-possession of royalty they cross to our circle and greet each of us in turn. We are not surprised. We are pleased to see them: they have come to help us understand.

The bear is a great scruffy beast, a mountain of an animal standing nearly four feet at the shoulder. From his size and his arching profile we surmise that he is a grizzly. Slow-moving, carrying his huge mass with the forbearance of a weary redcap, he has the markings of great age: his brown fur is dull and flecked with gray, his moon face and barrel nose nearly white. Motionless for seconds in the orange light, he then drops his massive head to the duff. Solemnly he sniffs at the ground, a habit of his race which, like the scale and the meter stick, is designed to measure the earth. He wheels slowly, then with a snort and a deep sigh lowers himself to the ground beside the fire.

The wolf too seems an ancient animal. Her silver eyes are lustrous and searching, but her legs are spindly, her gait heavy with years. Her ribs show faintly through her matted ashen fur, yet her bearing tells of the grace and strength and verve that once hurled her like a blizzard at her startled prey and bore her home on leaps as tall as snowdrifts. She settles regally beside the bear and eyes us all. Her companion too turns from face to face, and then grows still and pensive. A moment passes and then the old bear speaks.

"Have you listened to the music of the river?" he asks dreamily. His yellow eyes gleam in the firelight. His voice is coarse as sandstone, soft and low as the rush of a summer wind.

There are nods all around. Old Bear smiles. He hums a jovial tune, his head bobbing rhythmically, his body swaying. The easy tumble of the river, which had blended unnoticed into the night, lifts abruptly out of the darkness and carries through the trees. While we listen, bedazzled, the Gila rises up in a great music, a riversong, a song of the story of life. At first we hear just a trickle, a piper tripping through the highlands. But soon it is joined by the leaping melodies of mountain brooks, the grand and rich sonorities of cataracts and whirlpools, and it flows ever faster, ever more inexorably toward realization in the great waters on the distant horizon. The music takes on many characters, now simple and clear, now riotous, now meandering. And yet a pattern underlies it all. No matter what the surge or swell, serenity returns, and a moment comes when the river once again winds gently through the greenwood, inspiring foolish daydreams in all who lie peaceably on her banks. The riversong is a song of the continuity of all life, of the intermingling of atoms high on the mountain with those that lie deep in the valley. The river touches us all, the bass and the pickerel who take her oxygen through the thin membranes of their gills, the oak and the box elder whose roots absorb her nourishment, the tuff and the rhyolite who taste her when she falls as rain, the cougar and the bobcat who take her in long cool swallows into their bellies. Even through the winter freeze the river does not forget: the story of life resonates forever within her molecules. The tumbling of her ice is a tumbling of her spirit— like the song of the gentler seasons, a song of wonder and excitement, a song of exultation.

The melody winds to a close. The music recedes into the night. In the distance it dips, then slips smoothly into the everyday murmur of the river.

Old Bear and Gray Wolf seem lost in reverie.

"For anyone who has known the Gila," says Old Bear, "the song of the river forever echoes in the heart."

"And of course there is also No River," declares Gray Wolf, her voice warm and soothing but more solemn than the bear's. "No River is the balancing force that too is a stanza in the Gila's song." She glances at her paw, and suddenly I recall the tiny bugs, and the streaks the color of cayenne pepper . . .

"It is so easy to walk carelessly in the forest," muses Gray Wolf. "Look—" She lifts her paw, and with that each of us feels compelled to glance at our own hands. "A streak of blood, a reminder of the meek and the small and the powerless. A manifestation of the life quanta that inhabit each measure of space around us. A sign that warns us of our strength and of the helplessness of small things. It reminds us, too, of our savagery, for it is so difficult to protect the weak from harm. But this mark affirms that it is well to try, for the river of life is continuous, and what we do to the small things we do also to ourselves. Each breath we take, each thought, each movement of a paw is the beginning of a wave that ripples outward across boundless space till the end of time, intersecting each atom of matter along its path. Such a terrible thing is easy to forget—it is our nature to do so! The tiny creatures are always there to remind us."

The darkness is now complete. The power of the fire joins us together. Suddenly we burst into a flurry of questions—one of us asks about the rocks, another the flowers, a third the trees. The animals turn to each other, pleased that we have entered into the spirit of the night.

"So many questions!" exclaims Gray Wolf. "Perhaps in the manner of Linnaeus we should divide your inquiry into smaller parts." Smiling, she turns to Old Bear. He gathers his thoughts for a moment and then begins.

"Flowers are where beauty is born. Each part of the flower is a nursery where something of beauty is conceived and nurtured before it journeys out into the world. Grace, for example, begins in the stamens, harmony in the anthers, radiance in the petals, splendor in the calyx, delicacy in the ovaries, fairness in the pistil."

One of us, growing courageous, interrupts to suggest that it must be the bees, then, flitting from flower to flower, who are responsible for spreading beauty throughout the world.

Old Bear smiles. "Not really," he says politely. "You're thinking of pollination. No, beauty is spread quite simply by sight, by smell, by feel—by all thirteen senses, really. When we encounter beauty we naturally take something from it, then give what remains a gentle push and send it on its way. Like the words that we use to speak to one another, beauty is a means of communication. Sometimes, during quarrels, during times of hatred and war, the language of beauty is silenced. At these times it does not disappear entirely from the world. Instead it takes temporary refuge in the flowers where it was born. There it remains, protected from malice, until it can safely venture out once more. Thus there is no need to worry that beauty will ever disappear, for, like matter and energy, beauty can never be destroyed. It will always be conserved, safe from harm, in the vigilant blossoms of the flowers."

"And the trees," says Gray Wolf. "Have you wondered why they are so grand and tall and proud? It is because trees have the responsibility for nurturing ideas in our world. Ideas begin in the earth below, in a dark horizon of humus and mineral matter. But when they are only germs they pass by capillary action into the roots of trees, along with water and mineral salts. They remain in the cambium, taking on richness and complexity, through the spring and summer. Then the sapwood begins to harden, and that is a signal, as when the shortening days of fall remind the birds that it is time to begin their migration. The fully developed ideas are now expired through the leaves and needles of the trees. They attach themselves to oxygen atoms and ride the wind until we breathe them in. In our heads the ideas manifest themselves as intuitions, strokes of genius, flashes of insight. They are quite complete when they leave the trees, but they need a mind to realize them. It's a partnership, you see."

Gray Wolf says to her companion, "You were going to tell about the rocks."

Old Bear nods but seems reluctant to begin. When finally he does it is in a voice suffused with melancholy.

"The rocks are where history is stored," he explains, gazing at the ground before him. "In the rocks are kept the memories, the stories of the earth." He turns to face the fire, now blinking low over the hot coals. "Recent events, stories we may need to get at quickly, those are stored in the softer rocks—the shales and the sandstones."

"Even in the soil itself," adds Gray Wolf.

"Now you can understand why we lie down at night. It is so that our heads will be as close to the earth as possible. In that way we are nearer the memories of our lives and the grand events of the ages. When we lie close to the earth, all of these can spring up and fill our heads and become the stuff of our dreams."

"Nesting in their trees so far from the ground, birds have very few dreams," observes Gray Wolf. "And while they are in flight they have almost no knowledge of their history."

"Some of them are quite silly," says Old Bear. "Short flights are not dangerous—I suppose they can even be quite enjoyable. But flights of any duration are passages from roots and traditions. That's why the idea of space travel and colonization of other planets is very foolish. To leave the earth is to reject the past, and to be without a past is to be empty. Those who leave the earth will wither like the leaves of autumn. The earth is our home."

"As for the more ancient histories," Gray Wolf goes on, "they are stored in the harder, igneous rocks—the granites and so on. Here are found the sagas, the legends, the myths that tell us who we are. Because so many new stories are born each day, new rocks must be formed continually to serve as repositories for them all. That explains the earthquakes and volcanoes—the Ring of Fire that circles our planet where the plates of the earth's crust grind together. When new rocks emerge they immediately absorb the day's events; the older ones slip downward with yesterday's in tow. If you look closely at a rock you can easily read its story—some thought or pleasantry, an image of a smile, the contours of a couple making love, the poem of the northern lights. All of them are there, each moment crystallized for all time—the history of our valley and our world."

She leans forward and places her long chin on the ground between her paws. "There is so much to tell," she says quietly.

"It is not possible for us to tell it all," Old Bear apologizes. "Each grain of sand is the story of a lifetime. The raindrops that teach us to dance, the thunder that is the strength of our convictions. You see, the Gila is a story that is reflected in the lives of each of us. The sunlight that is hope, the moonlight that is love . . ."

He stares off into space. I move to the fire and poke idly at the coals with a stick of wood. A brief flame surges, and suddenly I remember Goyathlay, the one they called Geronimo. I ask if he ever came to this spot in the forest.

Old Bear answers in a voice bright with excitement. "Oh, yes, he visited here often. He always came with several of his friends. They would lead their horses beside the river, listening attentively to the refreshing melody of the waters. When they reached here they would stop and tie their horses to a tree, and then Geronimo would visit with the golden columbine, *Aquilegia chrysantha*, one of the beings he loved most in the Gila. Geronimo knew that beauty is stored in the flower, and that the beauty stored in the golden columbine is the beauty of freedom. The word *columbine* comes from the Latin word for dove, and if you look at the flower you will clearly see five doves flying there. The petals like an eagle's talons give the columbine its genus name, from the Latin *aquila*, for eagle. This flower kept Geronimo free, for by loving it he was able to share in its power, the great power of the eagle and the dove. Even after he was captured he held the golden columbine forever in his thoughts, and thus he was always free.

"After he had greeted the columbine, Geronimo and his companions would throw off their clothes and dash to the grotto in the rocks. They would lie back in the warm waters and turn their eyes to the sky. Hours passed as they listened to the music of the river and absorbed the bright hope of the sun and took in the grand ideas of the pines and the sycamores. For all of this they thanked Usen, which was their name for God, for Allah, for Jehovah, for the One that fills the hearts of us all. They knew that Usen gives us the warm waters, the hope of the sun, the lovelight of the moon, the sweet and tender berries, the never-failing starlight, the laughter, the ecstasy of love, our little furry young . . ."

Old Bear's voice trails off into a whisper. He sighs, then scratches his head. "I am sorry, but I must rest now," he says quietly and closes his eyes.

The flames have winked out, and only a low bed of coals glows faintly in the darkness before us. Above us a breeze stirs, and into the clearing steals the first chill of night. Gray Wolf, who has been looking into the coals, now turns onto her side to face us.

"We must go soon," she says gently. "But I know that you have questions about the people, the ones they call the cliff dwellers. In the short time remaining I will tell you what I know of them, for their story is an important one for us all.

"These people inhabited the region for a thousand years before they moved up into the cliffs. They were shorter than today's people—the women averaged five feet, one inch, the men five feet, five inches."

Old Bear opens his eyes momentarily. "The men wore headbands," he says.

"From the moment of their arrival, these and other peoples throughout the lands of the Southwest dreamed of making their homes in the towering cliffs. It is easy to see why. Such habitation provides protection from harm, and the prospect is beautiful.

"But because of the dangers entailed in climbing the cliffs, the people continued to live on the flat earth in the manner of their ancestors. Some of them cut steps in the rock face, and in that way the young and the brave among them were able to climb the walls to explore the caves. To the old and the timid these courageous ones brought back stories of the fine discoveries they had made. But in the rains of autumn and the snows of winter the ascent was hazardous even for the brave ones, so for all these people the dream of living with the swallows in the clouds remained only a dream, a dream of a thousand years.

"Then something happened which often happens in our world. The people began to change in a direction in which they wanted to change. At first the metamorphosis was evident only in the wildest of the dreamers. Then the infectious energy of these few passed to the others, and soon all the people were affected. The cause of the change was a genetic mutation—not a random one like so many, but a directed one, a mutation that moved the people in a direction they desired with all their hearts. Once underway, the metamorphosis was swift; in only a few generations it was complete. And that was how the people came to have wings, and how they learned to fly to the cliffs like birds.

"Their dream come true, they set to work fashioning their dwellings in the canyon of inexpressible beauty. It seemed that they had found the perfect habitation, with the river singing below, the fertile uplands nearby where they could plant their corn and their beans, their impregnable dwellings in the tall cliffs where each morning they could be awakened by the hope-filled sun, and each night be put to sleep by the silver moon of love. Here they lived and raised their families for forty years, enjoying the peace and happiness of the valley, the wonderment of friendship, the stories by the fire, their little furry young.

"Then everything changed in a moment. An early winter came with cutting winds and black skies and miserable wet snowflakes the size of piñon cones. Among the people passed the certainty that all could not be well. One night their leader, a woman of great age named Luora, had a dream, and in her dream she saw that a calamity would befall her and her people if they remained in their sky homes on the Gila. In Luora's dream she saw the great blue waters that lie far to the east, and riding the waters a thousand ships, and sailing each ship a thousand men, each speaking a strange loud tongue, and each with skin the color of pale milkweed. And then the dream faded and a new one appeared, and Luora saw clearly the high desert country to the east and the mountain she had seen as a child, the mountain they now call Oscura Peak. In her dream Luora saw her people falling down at her feet, and their eyes boiling, and their skin turning black and slowly peeling from their bodies, till all were reduced to dust and bones. And this was because of a great blinding light that Luora saw in her dream, a light that blotted out the day, a light brighter than a thousand suns. But unlike the true sun, which is the bringer of hope, these thousand suns were the bringers of despair.

"And that was how Luora came to know that she and the others must leave the home they loved so much, and spread out among the peoples of the earth, carrying with them a message of peace and a conviction that a single sun must one day reign again. Thus it was that, in the days that followed, Luora's people said goodbye to their dwellings in the cliffs and to each other, and in twos and threes set out into the world with their message and their conviction. Now nearly seven centuries have passed, and the descendants of Luora's people have spread to the farthest corners of the earth. So much time, and yet their mission has not changed: they are still the messengers of peace."

The last coals of the fire blink out as Gray Wolf finishes her tale. Ebony night envelops us. A harsh wind shudders down the canyon. The wolf and the bear have vanished from our sight, and when Gray Wolf speaks next she is a disembodied voice in the darkness.

"It is late," she says. "Bear and I must go, for we are tired."

I can hear the labored breathing of the grizzly and sense that he has risen to his feet. One of us asks if they can stay the night.

Neither answers for a moment. Then the weary voice of Old Bear breaks the silence. "You must know that we cannot stay," he says. "The forest is no longer our home. We live far up among the rocks, where the singing of the river will not disturb our sleep."

They bid us a warm good night. We cannot see the animals but we know that they are passing swiftly from our presence and in a moment they will be gone. And then I remember, and at the last moment I call out. "The mountains," I say. "What about the mountains?"

A wondrous silence rises up from the cold earth. I strain my eyes, trying to make out a familiar form. But there is nothing—no light, no smell, not even the melody of the river to lend shape or substance to the night. With a start I realize that I am alone in the forest.

And then I sense an overwhelming presence, and I know that Old Bear has returned—Old Bear, who knows the mountains best. Although I cannot see him I know that his great head looms before me and that his great black nose is only inches from my face. I can smell his animal smell and hear his breathing and feel his chill breath upon my cheek, and I know that I am no longer alone.

And then I see the serene light glowing in the darkness before me. And it is in his beaming eyes, and it is moonlight glimmering on snow.

At daybreak we packed for the long journey home. Under cloud-speckled skies we followed the river to its intersection with the trail to the canyon rim. By noon we had reached our car, and by early evening we were reunited with the cat Magoo, who at first feigned indifference to our return. Soon, however, he was happily lapbound, deeply engrossed in our tales of the untamed Gila.

Several weeks later, I was out walking near the university when I noticed an Indian woman approaching me on the sidewalk. She seemed to be in her early twenties, a woman of enchanting beauty whose eyes had the dazzle of a midsummer sun. She was wearing a long skirt and a bright cotton blouse, both embroidered in a red-and-black diamond pattern that I recognized as traditional among the Pueblo women of Acoma.

Smiling softly, humming to herself, she caught my eye as she passed. I had slowed my pace at her approach and now, meaning no disrespect, I turned to watch as she continued on her way. I admired her for a moment and was about to resume my walk when I noticed something unusual—a slight movement under her blouse, a rustling of what appeared to be a pair of bony forms, like folded arms. And, peeking out beneath, a fleck of downy white.

Wings, as sure as I have eyes. Wings for flying home.

Decrescendo

Long ago, in Kentucky, I, a boy, stood
By a dirt road, in first dark, and heard
The great geese hoot northward.

I could not see them, there being no moon
And the stars sparse. I heard them.
ROBERT PENN WARREN, *"Tell Me a Story"*

Toward sundown, as a cold, wind-driven January afternoon hastened to a close in the ancient flat-topped mountains of north-central Colorado, the snow cloud that had gripped the upper ramparts of Castle Peak for most of the day drew away, and I caught my first clear glimpse of the summit rocks. In that revealing moment I remembered the howl of Old Lefty. It was a shock to recollect that unearthly sound, because I had never heard the howl of a wild wolf before—certainly not the howl of Old Lefty, who by the time I was born had been dead twenty years, one of the last wild wolves in the Colorado Rockies. But I remembered it clearly, the way you remember the rhythm of a childhood verse, or the cadence of your father's voice, or the energy of a long-lost Benny Goodman record . . . hollow, floating, ghostly, slowly rising, cracking, then settling in somewhere far above your head, white-hot, the color of fever. The howl an old Pennsylvania trapper once likened to the sound of a dozen train whistles, and Grizzly Adams, in a more conventional rendering, called a horrible noise, the most hateful a man alone in the wilderness at night can hear.

I was standing in a snowy garden of sagebrush when I remembered the call. Above me, deep organ tones of twilight rumbled off the rocky turrets that gave the peak its name. In 1921, with a suitcase full of Number 4½ Newhouse traps under his arm and a .30-30 on his shoulder, government hunter Bert Hegewa came out from Denver on an urgent mission for the United States Biological Survey. Somewhere near here, at about this time of year—courting season, high howling season—he imposed officially sanctioned silence on the clamorous slopes of Castle Peak. With that, wolves were effaced forever from Castle Peak, from the White River National Forest, from all the great Rockies of this majestic quarter of Colorado.

Or so people thought. Yet the feverish cry stayed on. Sixty-eight years later, on a wolf hunt of my own, I heard it again, soaring high above the mountain, clear as a sky-gram of snow geese. Silence is long but memory is longer, and even the forgetful have flashbacks.

Sound is a wave. Unlike light waves, which can traverse empty space, a sound wave requires a medium—a solid, a liquid, or a gas—if it is to travel. As the wave moves, the particles of the medium vibrate along the axis of the direction of travel, alternately bunching together and separating. The number of bunches, or cycles, that pass a given point in one second is the frequency of the wave. Human ears can hear frequencies from a low of about 16 cycles per second—a little below the lowest note on a piano—to a high of about 20,000, a nearly inaudible hissing or rasping sound. It is natural to imagine that if we cannot sense something it must not exist, but the bounteousness of sound provides a good palliative to that conceit. One creature's silence may be another's serenade. Bats are expert composers of ultrasonic waves, their shouts and whispers reaching frequencies of 120,000 cycles per second. Listen some evening to a spirited gathering of bats and you may wonder what all the fuss is about; the bulk of their chatter will be lost to your ears, pitched far beyond the range of your hearing.

Wolves, on the other hand, because they can hear at least partway into this confab, might prick up their ears. To you, a quiet evening on Castle Peak; to a wolf, pandemonium.

How an ear that has never heard the howl of a wolf can remember it has not been determined. The Sioux prophet Black Elk gave us one possible explanation. "I did not have to remember these things," he said of the particulars of the great vision he had received sixty years earlier. "They have remembered themselves all these years."

Then, too, there are people who seem to be born with sounds in their heads—those with perfect pitch, for example, who can sing any musical note at will by calling it up from the complete library of tones they carry around in their minds. Where they collected these handy melodies none of them can explain. Perhaps precision-tuned pitch pipes are included among the toys that our proud genes can select for us as baby gifts, along with silver spoons, green thumbs, and the rest. Perhaps wolf howls are the same, bright packages from the Pleistocene, memories of nights when the howl of a wolf was a signal to sleep lightly and draw closer to the flames.

The cause is uncertain, but not the effect: toward sundown on a frosty January afternoon, it is possible to stand on a silent mountainside that has not known the song of a wolf for sixty-eight years and to hear it again, sharply, like a pandemonium of bats.

The intensity of a sound is a function of the amplitude of the sound wave. At each end of the spectrum of intensity there is a celebrant in nature. The ocean is loud; the desert is quiet. The ocean inspires sermons and symphonies; the desert, contemplation and introspection.

The mountain traveler encounters both extremes and everything in between. A mountain is thunder and sunrise, waterfall and hoarfrost, thrush song and juniper. A visitor to the high country is rocked continually from one end of the curve to the other. On the north slope of Castle Peak I tracked a rabbit upward through the snow for the better part of an hour; I stopped when the scream of the wind, a sure counterpoise to the silent tracks, told me I had gone high enough. A mountain broadcasts in full-dimensional stereo, and every wavelength has something to say.

I had set out on Lefty's trail at sunup that morning, driving north from Interstate 70 on a country road that ambled along beside the Colorado River into a broad valley cleaving two sections of the White River National Forest. Where the road tunneled through shadow, islands of black cinder-ice corrugated the surface. But despite the season, the wide floodplain of the river was mostly bare of snow, and the Colorado itself, just a peppy stream in this early chapter of its travels, had opened a confident course through the ice. Angling up from the river to the east were the lower ramparts of Castle Peak, mile-wide buttresses splintered by dark, nasty-looking gullies. The rock was pink and sorrel and shattered, stacked crazily like overdue library books, dotted with piñon and cedar. Here on the outskirts of the Rockies the land felt dusty and sunbaked, even in winter. The valley moved with a slow, primordial pulse, a rhythm of giant ferns and dinosaurs.

For more than a century this has been cattle country, and any hunt for wolves here must include a hunt for ranchers. In a hundred miles of wandering on rocky roads encircling Castle Peak I found just one man who remembered wolves. He was eighty-four. For most of his life he had run cattle in the valley, as his father had before him. Wolves were gone by the time he took up the trade. Nevertheless, mention of this ancient nemesis, after the slaughterhouse perhaps the most efficient killer of cattle and sheep, brought no faraway look to his eyes. He hadn't seen wolves in seventy years and that wasn't a day too long. I asked him about Old Lefty, and he said he remembered a renegade

wolf and valley ranchers hiring a trapper to clear it out, probably while
he was still a teenager. But when I asked him if he remembered the
wolf's howl he shook his head. I saw that if I was going to find Lefty I'd
have to do it on my own, so around noon I parked the car in a grove of
cedar where the dirt road turns left toward McCoy, packed a lunch, and
took off cross-country toward the summit of Castle Peak. My plan was
to spend the afternoon paying my respects, exploring the bluffs and ravines Lefty had known so well, perhaps turning up a relic of his twelve
years on the mountain. But it wasn't long after leaving the car that I'd
forgotten my plan and was prowling after rabbit tracks, listening to the
wind.

Silence is not "nothing." Only a person who is permanently and totally
unconscious hears nothing; to the rest of us, silence communicates
content and evokes an emotional response. Think of the pregnant
pause, the calm before the storm, the eloquence of Harpo Marx, the
working silence of a Quaker meeting, the shouting silence of a Beckett
play. Look at Edvard Munch's *Scream*, and listen. Think of what Jack
Benny could do with silence, the most lethal weapon in his considerable comedic arsenal. Think of the music the audience hears in John
Cage's notorious $4'33''$, as the players sit through the piece without lifting their instruments. Think of the knockout physical power of silence. Mathematics writer Martin Gardner reported that once, as a
practical joke on the conductor of a symphony orchestra, the members
of the orchestra agreed to fall silent in the middle of a strident compo-
sition. At the prearranged moment the musicians abruptly stopped
playing, and the conductor fell off the podium.

Silence can have less violent but equally remarkable physical effects. During the silence of meditation people's hearts slow and their
blood pressure drops. In the Sudan, the Mabaans have perfected a
method of hunting that is based on complete silence; as a result, the
noise level of their everyday speech has dropped so low that it is practically inaudible to outsiders. Mabaans move softly, as graceful as

dancers, and are said to conduct themselves in a composed and amiable manner. When they hunt, they can hear animals no one else knows to be there.

The sound of America was wild, and it was ear-rending. Listen:

Pelicans, ditzy wing-slappers, rising by the hundreds like a clatter of pots and pans over the river islands of places we know today as Kansas and Nebraska. Parakeets, shrieking flocks of them, in Virginia, Tennessee, and the Carolinas, tame, darting, pint-size rainbows swarming inches from the fingertips. Turkeys jabbering, jammed so thickly into trees along the river banks of Arkansas, Missouri, and Oklahoma that travelers told of turkey trees and likened the birds to apples. Whooping cranes tall as trombones, tooting their five-foot windpipes across Louisiana, Iowa, New Jersey, and Maryland. Trumpeter swans, elegant thirty-pound jazz bands, blaring down the Ohio and the Mississippi and south to the Gulf. Ivory-billed woodpeckers, monstrous wild-eyed things, red-crested, hard-hatted, jackhammering the forests of Georgia, South Carolina, Florida, and Alabama. Plovers and curlews, shrill-crying, roaming the Atlantic like storm clouds, pounding the mainland of Massachusetts, Rhode Island, Connecticut, and New York. And for 9 million years, sandhill cranes, too high to be seen, too clamorous to go unheard, passing over Nebraska, over the Southwest and the Midwest, over all the Atlantic states.

The living wind—the words are Aldo Leopold's—of passenger pigeons. Six miles off, a flock had as good as arrived: the wind shifted, the horizon purred. Then a roar and a blacking out of the sun for hours and sometimes days as the birds flew by. John James Audubon, that master statistician, estimated 300 million birds per hour in one passing flock. Such a throng didn't nest, it besieged several hundred square miles of trees, took them over like paratroopers. At night the sound of their gargantuan bickering made the forest crackle and hum as though it were afire.

Walruses, fat and bossy, fussy as bankers, bleating dawn to dusk on the rocky shores of Maine and Massachusetts. Prairie dogs, squat and sassy, jabbering from Kansas to the Gulf of Mexico, a 500-mile-long salute to small talk. Screeching squirrels by the tens of thousands, migrating across the plains in dense, relentless columns. At a river, at the Missouri or the Platte, the first brigade would plunge in and drown, the second would take to the backs of the first and race across. Gold-coated, deep-throated jaguars, gliding through Tennessee, Arkansas, Oklahoma, and New Mexico. Bighorns cracking heads from Canada to Mexico, grizzlies bawling in every corner of the West, mountain lions hissing and screaming in Rhode Island, in Delaware.

Bison herds of ten thousand in Kentucky. On the plains the total ran to 30 or 40 million. Large herds measured twenty-five miles end to end and numbered a quarter-million animals. George Catlin likened the sound of unseen bison to that of distant thunder. Meriwether Lewis wrote of the continuous roar of hundreds of males battling at once during mating season, a trampling and bellowing audible six miles away.

And everywhere, in Vermont and Utah, in Iowa and Nevada, in the Dakotas, Pennsylvania, Wisconsin, Oregon, and West Virginia, on the plains, in the mountains, on the tundra and the desert, the haunting, floating cry of the animals whose range exceeded all others: the resonant, scintillating, sepulchral howling of wolves.

For several hours I improvised a raggedy theme-and-variations that wandered generally upward along the north and west slopes of Castle Peak. Unlike the forbidding fourteen-thousand-foot peak of the same name near Aspen, Lefty's Castle is a home, a gentle and welcoming place, the kind of mountain that even in January invites you to come up and stay awhile. The theme for the day was Lefty, but since I wasn't sure how to elaborate it I let the variations discover themselves. For a time I followed the rabbit tracks, which bounded along before me as breezily and expertly as Arthur Murray dance prints. Suddenly they disappeared into thin air.

Houdini, this bunny. How did he do it? Midway across an acre of cottony snow the confident prints, racing smartly for the far edge, simply up and ended.

I knelt to inspect the evidence, silent but certainly not mute. Maybe he forgot something, executed a flying 180, and scampered home in the original tracks. But the positioning of the toes told me otherwise: this was a one-way street. Searching the gray sky to the west, I spotted a red-tailed hawk barrel-rolling high over the valley of the Colorado. I'd been told that those fellows sometimes tackle rabbits. Hypothesis: frisky Peter was not Houdini at all, but hare-brained Icarus.

Abandoned by my faithful guide, I momentarily felt lost. I looked toward the top of the mountain and heard the wind whistling a not-so-silent warning to stay below. The chill summit rocks disappeared beneath a restless cloud. About me the aroma of sage, until now a lively companion on my travels, went bitter and cheerless.

I turned and adjusted my focus thirty miles, to Dome Peak, white and spectacular on the horizon. Suddenly I thought of my friend Art. We climbed together for a decade, traversed a hundred slopes like this one to reach the soaring summit routes we favored. We were first on the airy crest of Mount Russell one spring, the year his brother died of cancer. On that dizzy, snowbound eminence I saw him kneel, slip the notebook from the summit canister, and write, "This one's for Jim." We joked about the Himalaya and the Far North, and I promised him that one day before too long I would phone him and say, "Let's go." And that would mean it was time for us to take a deep breath and head for Nepal.

He walked me off the Grand Teton the day I quit, the day I decided that twenty years was enough, that, because I was afraid, I must never tie a rope around my waist again. He took me to his tent on the Lower Saddle, in a disturbing and disorienting amber light. In the hush of the mountains, we talked for an entire afternoon about my shame and heartbreak, and about a new and unanticipated disorder, the deadly emptiness I felt. Art helped me through the ordeal as we had often helped each other over a difficult section of a climb.

To my surprise he told me of his own fears, the quaking knees at the tough spots, the midnight premonitions that the next mountain would be his last. I went home to a new life without climbing. He continued, but not for long. A few months later, on a route called Ordeal on Discovery Wall at Pinnacles National Monument in California, his waist harness somehow became disengaged from the rope. He fell a hundred feet to his death.

I couldn't join my friends when they carried the tiny package of ashes to Mount Moran in the Tetons, because it would have violated my vow. But a few days later in the shining High Sierra I scrambled to the top of amiable Shepherd Crest, a mountain designed for the new me, and there, alone on a grand, million-mile afternoon, I spoke the words of the Hundred and Twenty-first Psalm: "I will lift up mine eyes unto the hills, from whence cometh my help"; then I knelt, slipped the notebook from the canister, and penciled in my gift: "This one's for Art."

In the late afternoon, bumblebee-sized snowflakes began darting on the wind. A sudden gust hurtled out of Bull Gulch and caught me on the open slope just below Castle Creek Ponds. I stopped and pulled on my mittens. This was as high as I would go today, not much over nine thousand feet, still two thousand below the summit. I had thought of going to the top, but the summit cloud had deterred me and, perhaps semi-deliberately, I had dawdled too long on my errands. Today the top of Castle Peak seemed a poor idea for someone alone.

But I was not alone. A hundred feet higher and a few degrees to my right, an almost imperceptible flutter in the sagebrush caught my eye. A lithe doe, her gossipy tail twittering, moved out of a shadow, paused, then sprang effortlessly up the slope as though carried by the breeze. She stopped and tilted her nose upward. I could see her twitching flanks, the thin puffs of smoke at her nostrils. We both came swiftly to attention, and I wondered what she perceived in the silence of the snowfall.

She sprang again. I gasped in surprise as behind her the graceful, unexpected parade bounded into view: a second zigzagging in her hoofprints, then a third and a fourth and a fifth. In a handsome line the quintet danced along the ridgeline above me, blithe captives of an unheard song.

We can say with some confidence that prior to 1850 there must have been several thousand wolves in Colorado. True country squires, they had an easy time of it, feeding on a seemingly inexhaustible supply of bison, pronghorn, deer, and other natural prey with which they shared the mountains and the plains.

In 1858 the balance that had obtained for thousands of years began to totter. In the fall of that year a teamster turned loose a few old oxen in the eastern part of the state, assuming the animals would starve over the winter. Instead they happened onto rich winter grass. The following spring the oxen turned up fat and healthy.

A few years later a settler named Sam Hartsel confirmed the discovery. He drove a hundred head of shorthorn cattle into the high mountain park west of Colorado Springs and there found hardy grasses flourishing year-round. At precisely the moment when less imaginative entrepreneurs were pouring into Colorado in search of prosaic silver and gold, cowmen hit a mother lode of far greater and more lasting importance to the state's economy: Sam Hartsel struck grass, and the rush was on to graze the Rockies.

To justify clearing the land for settlement, we turned to the myths that had served us faithfully on each step of the march west. Duty and destiny stood foremost—vindications since Plymouth. Then there were more finely tuned romances, each with its own local slant. The myth of the evil wolf, for example, a favorite since Aesop, found a ready home in Colorado. By 1870, stock tales of "cruel," "ruthless," and "bloodthirsty" wolves that preferred steak to all other meat were staples of Colorado folklore.

But to excuse the massacre of prairie dogs, bison, bighorn sheep, and other docile creatures, animals even the most messianic booster couldn't tag as evil, we required more upbeat delusions. We turned to two American classics, the myths of the mighty hunter and of the people who loved the land.

The first had its genesis in eighteenth-century Kentucky: Daniel Boone in buckskin—brave, crafty, persevering, the wily natural man alone against the beasts of the forest. After the Civil War we added a grand and irrefutable subtext to the basic narrative, one obedient to the new god, Technology. We might wince at shooting raccoons and porcupines, but the hallowed names of Winchester, Springfield, Sharps, Henry, Spencer, and a host of other distinguished arms manufacturers quickly relieved us of our pesky misgivings. After all, their products gleamed with American ingenuity, which was Heaven-sent. Besides, those wondrous engines—breech-loaders, magazine loaders, telescopic sights, smokeless powder, all manner of poisons and traps— were handsome, well-made, practical, efficient; we'd be fools not to use them!

Every region had its own local Buffalo Bill, a hero who cleared the woods of one pest or another. The inheritance of these mighty hunters exalted them; technology made them divine.

It was, as I say, a myth. The hunters who cleared America of wildlife during the nineteenth century did very little hunting, and they did not need to be particularly brave, since the greatest danger most of them faced during their tramps in the woods was that their rifles might explode in their faces or they might swallow some of their own poison. The great American hunt for wild animals was more like a lazy swing on the front porch with a mint julep by your side. Pigeon hunters kindled sulfur fires under the trees of nesting passenger pigeons. The fumes rose up; the birds plopped dead onto the ground. Those that flew away before succumbing to the fumes slammed into nets or phalanxes of swinging poles wielded by the fire builders, who then picked up the downed birds and crushed their heads with pincers.

On the plains, bison hunters perfected the still-hunt. Standing in place, the hunter first hunted for a bison, not much of a challenge since in all likelihood he was facing several thousand of the animals languidly munching on prairie grass. Having selected his target, he next hunted for the choicest spot on thirty square feet of stationary bison hide at which to aim his bullet. After firing, he waited patiently while other bison gathered around the dead animal in curiosity, then hunted for the choicest spot at which to aim on each of them.

When the animal did not come to the hunter, the hunter hunted not for the animal but for a clever place to hide his traps and his poisons. Traps were riskier, since a trapped animal could escape by chewing off its snared limb. Poison quickly became the weapon of choice for hunters during the land-clearing decades of the last century (and, indeed, remains so for state and federal hunters today). Unlike the trap, which provided an out for any animal gutsy or crazed enough to mutilate itself, poison left nothing to chance. Poison carried the cachet of authority, of the final word. Poison was *democratic*—that was what moved the heart. Strychnine, the most popular, in notably hideous fashion killed not only the animal that consumed it but every animal that fed on the newly created carcass, and on their carcasses, and so on down the line. Not only wolves and coyotes, the principal targets, but eagles, hawks, owls, skunks, woodchucks, prairie dogs, squirrels, dogs, cats, horses, goats, and occasionally children consumed strychnine on the great land and died. Stanley Young, a supervisor with the U. S. Biological Survey who oversaw the killing of some of the last wild wolves in the West (and who was, paradoxically, one of the first persons to take a scientific interest in the wolf), reported that no rancher ever passed up a dead animal without lacing it with a liberal dose of strychnine.

Poison on the land: we arrive at the second of our great national delusions, that of the people who loved the land. To appreciate the myth fully, keep vividly before you a picture of a mass of strychnine on a grand expanse of nineteenth-century America and, around it, scores of gruesomely twitching beasts. As they convulse in their death throes, consider this people who loved the land, these pioneers rapturous before the majestic plains and mountains, these ranchers and farmers in the red sunset kneeling reverently to the ground and sifting the sweet-smelling earth between their fingers.

I do not know how to see it except as myth. The belief that we loved the land is central to our vision of ourselves as a people. Yet that treasured belief, so necessary if we were to transform the land into the subservient habitation we know today, fails entirely to square with the evidence. Certainly we loved something—the idea of the land, the promise of the land. But the land was forests, which we leveled, and topsoil, which we destroyed, and rivers, which we dammed, and streams, which we polluted, and grasses, which we burned, and swamps, which we drained, and Indians, whom we decimated, and wildlife, which we massacred. That is the record, and it does not sound like love.

A poison was on the land. And the poison was this: *This land will make you rich*.

Nineteenth-century literature abounds in tales of hunting adventure, much of it quite rapid:

One second in the life of John James Audubon:
Weapon: rifle and one bullet
Take: seven whooping cranes

Forty minutes in the life of Thomas C. Nixon:
Weapon: rifle
Take: 120 bison

One day in the life of Frank M. Stahl and friends:
Weapons: rifles
Take: forty wolves

One day in the life of a Natchez, Mississippi, hunter:
Weapon: rifle
Take: 750 golden plover

One night in the life of two Kansas Territory hunters:
Weapon: strychnine
Take: sixty-four wolves

One day in the life of George W. Brown:
Weapon: strychnine
Take: thirteen wolves, fifteen coyotes, forty skunks

One day in the life of Windham Thomas Wyndham-Quin, Fourth
    Earl of Dunsraven:
Weapon: rifle
Take: 120 woodland caribou

One year in the life of Robert Peck:
Weapon: strychnine
Take: 800 wolves

One year in the life of the residents of Sun City, Kansas Territory:
Weapons: miscellaneous
Take: enough wolves to pave a road seventy-five yards wide with the
    carcasses

Eighteen months in the life of William Cody:
Weapon: .50-70 Springfield Army musket
Take: 4,280 bison

Three years in the life of Sir St. George Gore:
Weapon: rifle
Take: 105 bear, 1,600 elk and deer, more than 2,000 bison

By 1870 the bison, the principal prey of the wolf, was stampeding toward oblivion. Bison hunter William Webb estimated that, in 1871, hunters shot 50,000 bison in Kansas and Colorado alone. Hunters sometimes took hides and tongues, but the bulk they left to rot on the plains. Webb put the amount of abandoned bison meat from these 50,000 kills at 20 million pounds. Bison carcasses were said to line the Kansas Pacific Railroad route for 200 miles.

The slaughter continued through the following decade, with hunters complaining that the numbers of animals at which to shoot were
decreasing steadily. By 1885, hunters actually had to hunt for bison. By
the turn of the century, 75 million of the animals were dead, 999,999
out of every million that had lived. A few dozen remained.

Other species had fared little better, and some worse. Grizzlies had
been extirpated from 99 percent of their former range in the contiguous United States. Plover and curlew no longer filled the Atlantic sky.
The turkey trees were gone, as were the clattering pelicans of Kansas
and Nebraska, the walruses of New England, the jaguars of Tennessee,
Arkansas, Oklahoma, and New Mexico, the mountain lions of Delaware and Rhode Island. Sandhill cranes, whooping cranes, and trumpeter swans hung on by a thread (those seven whooping cranes Audubon killed with one bullet were one-third of all the whooping cranes
alive in 1941). The megalopolis of prairie dogs had disappeared. Bri-
gades of squirrels no longer migrated over the plains. The magnitude
of the disaster is impossible to comprehend, but in *Of Wolves and
Men*, Barry Lopez's magnificent biography of the wolf, Lopez puts as
carefully calculated a number on it as we are ever likely to get. From
1850 to 1900, he estimates, some 500 million creatures were killed in
the United States. Perhaps it is enough to say that by the turn of the century, the raucous cry of the American wilderness had been reduced to
a gravelly, consumptive whisper.

A few species—Eastern elk, Labrador duck, sea mink—had disappeared altogether. But most held on into the new century. Then the
amazing completeness of the rout, and the irreversibility, became
blindingly manifest. Merriam's elk winked out in 1906, Badlands bighorn in 1910, Louisiana parakeets in 1912, Carolina parakeets in
1914, Wisconsin cougar and California grizzly bears in 1925, ivory-
billed woodpeckers, probably, in 1946. The last passenger pigeon, a female named Martha, died in the Cincinnati Zoo in 1914.

As their traditional prey disappeared, wolves turned their attention
to domestic stock. For a short time they prospered. But as cattle and

sheep losses mounted through the latter decades of the nineteenth century, ranchers and local governments committed themselves to the total eradication of wolves. With bounties as incentives, with rifles, traps, and poisons as their tools, hunters set upon the wolf with a ferocity unmatched in the annals of a notably ferocious war, one rooted not in annoyance, the charge against species that were merely in the way, or contempt, the curse on the ridiculous bison, but in hatred and rage. Barry Lopez estimates the harvest at between one and two million wolves. By 1915, when the federal government chipped in with $125,000 to clear wolves from federal lands, including the national parks, only a handful of renegades remained in the lower forty-eight states.

Above and slightly to the left of the famous orange-red supergiant Betelgeuse in the constellation of Orion, in the relatively empty region where ancient peoples pictured the raised right arm of the hunter, there shines a star of medium brightness known to astronomers as 75 Orionis. It is about 125 light years from Earth, which means that a beam of light setting out from 75 Orionis will rocket the frozen darkness of interstellar space for about 125 years before touching down on this planet.

It works both ways. One hundred twenty-five years after an event unfolds on Earth, the optical record of that event will arrive in the vicinity of 75 Orionis. Thus, sometime in the next few years, snoopy astronomers on a lush blue-green planet that we might imagine to be orbiting the star at a safe and civilized distance can turn their telescopes on Earth and watch as Thomas C. Nixon kills 120 bison in forty minutes; not long after that, they can take in the night-long dispatching of sixty-four wolves by poisoning, courtesy of two Kansas Territory hunters, and a few months later the one-day slaughter of 120 woodland caribou by Windham Thomas Wyndham-Quin, Fourth Earl of Dunsraven.

The views, then, from deep space are spectacular. Not so the music.

Because space is a vacuum, the silence of the cosmos is complete and unbreakable. (A few reclusive atoms do pop up out there every once in a while, but not enough to carry a tune.) Were someone to go for a float with me out near 75 Orionis and to turn to me to comment on the lovely view—perhaps the curious new perspective on the Milky Way, or the handsome grain on the stock of Lord Dunsraven's rifle—I wouldn't hear the remark. Were my companion to shout, I wouldn't hear. Were my friend, in frustration at my failure to respond, to line up ten cement mixers, a hundred jumbo jets, and a thousand rock concerts (or, more to the point, one to two million wolves) and set them all howling at once, I would hear nothing. We are not considering a variation on the old paradox of the tree falling silently in the forest, which depends on an absence of ears; here there are ears but there are no gabby particles vibrating in a medium for them to hear.

It is not sufficient to call this silence. Unlike the pregnant pause, the silence of Harpo Marx, or the calm before the storm, this is a consummate silence, a silence without dreams, a silence known only to the unconscious. Here in the emptiness of the northern sky we have discovered our ideal listening post, where we can sit back, kick off our shoes, and tune in to the immaculate voice of extinction.

On its nightly rounds sometime in 1913, a four-year-old male gray wolf, the alpha wolf of one of the last wild packs in Colorado, stepped into a steel trap concealed in a clump of sagebrush somewhere on Castle Peak. The trap sprang, snaring the wolf by the left front leg. The wolf, which by all accounts appears to have been an unusually determined animal, chewed its own flesh and bone through to the core, and some hours or days later it rejoined its pack. A rancher checking the trap afterward found the wolf's severed left forefoot.

The stub of the wounded leg soon healed and, with what ranchers in the Castle Peak region began to understand as premeditated malice, the pack resumed its nightly business. The lead wolf learned to run on three legs, lowering the fourth to the ground only when leaping an ob-

stacle in its path. Every stockman in Eagle County learned to recognize the unmistakable signature. It soon became more than a set of
prints: it became a symbol of revenge. Ranchers found it, or thought
they found it, in the mess of tracks surrounding every freshly killed
sheep or steer. They believed that the wolf marked its kills with its personal stamp, like a serial killer.

Castle Peak was made a minefield of traps and poison pellets. But
somehow the killing went on. For some reason, traps and poisons had
no effect on the pack's depredations. Perhaps, as one of the last, the lead
wolf was one of the fittest—a wolf capable of learning a lesson from the
1913 disaster, an animal of uncommon vigilance and discrimination.

A remarkable animal, yes, but not the mythic beast that came into
being. Before long, local legend had elevated the hobbled wolf from
three-legged leader of the pack to phantom killer, a supernatural beast
striking in the dead of night, impervious to man's pathetic weapons.
During the eight years following the loss of its foot, the wolf was blamed
for the deaths of 384 head of livestock in the Castle Peak region. By
1921, when local ranchers threw in the towel and called for help from
the federal government, the legend of Old Lefty, the smartest, cussed-
est, most black-hearted wolf anyone in these parts had ever come up
against, was in full flower.

Help arrived in the person of Bert Hegewa. He moved into a one-
room cabin near the mouth of Bull Gulch on Castle Peak early in January 1921. Like most members of the mop-up team employed by the
U.S. Biological Survey, Hegewa was an anomaly, a hunter who really
knew how to hunt. He chalked up an impressive record against the wily
and tenacious wolves he stalked. A month earlier he had killed all the
members of a resolute pack near Pagoda Springs; during the previous
year, another dozen renegades. After finishing his business with Lefty,
he would kill a wolf called Unaweep on the Uncompahgre Plateau
near the Utah border, and after that Bigfoot, a wolf that had acquired a
chilling reputation as "the terror of the Lane Country."

In *The Last Stand of the Pack*, a 1929 work in which survey super-

visor Stanley Young documented the agency's work in stamping out the
last pockets of wolf resistance, Young left us a picture of Bert Hegewa:
about thirty years of age, of medium height, bearded, with tousled,
tawny hair and premature crow's feet around blue eyes. Hegewa went
about in a red-and-black checked woodsman's shirt and corduroy
pants, and he carried a .30-30 rifle. Young dedicated his book to Hegewa and the other hunters of the survey:

> They are the heirs of the Mountain Men. They are the followers of the
> last frontiers. They are the friends of all animals; the compassionate, re-
> gretful executioners of animal renegades when such outlaws must die
> that other wildlings may live.
> On far trails, wind swept, snow blanketed, hail pelted, on trails
> where frost bites or sun bakes, on trails where danger stalks with them as
> a close companion, these determined men carry on the tradition of the
> organization to which they belong. They get their wolf!

Hegewa spent his days exploring the wide slopes and shattered ravines of Castle Peak. Although the mountain is only 11,275 feet in
height, it is massive and complex, encompassing well over 60 square
miles of convoluted terrain above the eight-thousand-foot level. In two
weeks of trying, the hunter found not a trace of Lefty and his band.

One morning near mid-month, he awoke to a blizzard raging on the
summit of the mountain. Against the advice of a cowboy with whom
he shared the cabin, Hegewa took off on skis. He toured the mountain,
staying below the storm throughout the day. Once again he came up
empty-handed.

Then, toward sunset, just as he was about to head for home, he spotted faint animal tracks in the snow. The tracks led him up a draw and
over a ridge, into a thicket of mountain mahogany. Hegewa followed,
crossing a meadow, then skiing into a stand of yellow pine. There, out
of the wind, the faint marks became clear, and Hegewa found what he
had been looking for: the fresh signature of a wolf running on three
legs. The hunter guessed that the track was less than an hour old.

Night was falling and the blizzard had moved lower on the mountain. In a strong wind and heavy snowfall, Hegewa set out in pursuit of the wolf. Dusk found him on the south side of the mountain, climbing toward the center of the storm. At tree line the track leveled off, then descended into the shelter of the forest. Hegewa stayed with it till finally, in last light, he lost the trail.

But he had good reason to congratulate himself, for he had found the pack's main runway on the mountain. Now in full darkness, too far from the cabin to return in safety, he thrashed through the trees until he located a spruce with an inviting undercover of snow. He unlatched his skis, then, perhaps momentarily warmed by a glow of keen satisfaction, burrowed under the snow and prepared to spend a cold night out.

Sixty-eight years later, in an easier cold on a high vantage ground somewhere on Castle Peak, I danced from one foot to the other in a waggish effort to stay warm. Twilight lay softly on the mountain, bringing a transitory peace, like tower chimes. I peered down snowy slopes into the valley of the ebony Colorado. Wide fields crisscrossed by streams and fences glimmered in the half-light. Within them cattle stood and shuddered, anticipating the terrors of the night. Closer by, the deer grew still and rabbits turned to stone. The silent world was wolf country tonight.

I moved to the edge of a gulch, a shadowy rent in the mountainside tumbling ever wider toward the distant river. A wall of massive frost-hewn blocks shored up one side, its lengths and widths so masterfully rendered that for a moment I thought the wall was human-built.

I warmed at the thought. Then I peered down to the jumbled floor of the gulch falling into darkness and felt a chill. Suddenly I understood how far I had come to reach this place.

I had meant to be in Glenwood Springs by now. But at sunset the sky had cleared, the wind died down, and a perfect quiet crept in over the mountainside. It was a peace too rare to squander. I had no food or flashlight or extra clothing, but no matter; I would stay on awhile, tune in to the sound of night on Castle Peak.

I looked at the sky, wide open now, harbinger of an arctic night. The

first star flicked on and then the second, and soon the entire show. By
snowlight I contoured east in search of a suitable listening post among
the huddled sage. In the silvery light the yellow-green plants looked lu-
minous, the mountainside shone with the luster of satin.

Existence, preached Vladimir Nabokov, is but a brief crack of light
between two eternities of darkness. In his enchanting autobiography,
Speak, Memory, Nabokov tells the story of a young man of his acquain-
tance, a chronophobic Nabokov calls him, who saw home movies
taken a few weeks before his birth. The beloved house, his mother waving from an upstairs window, especially the empty baby carriage awaiting his arrival: these familiar sights possessed an existence that somehow excluded the man's own, and they threw him into a panic.
Nabokov writes that the man felt as if in the reverse course of events his
very bones had disintegrated. In that terrifying moment he witnessed
the perfect silence of deep space.

The daredevil in me is envious. But, denied prenatal docudramas
and interstellar joy rides, where am I to turn for such diversion? Perhaps to Aldo Leopold, who recommends "Thinking Like a Mountain." Leopold knew well the cry of the wild wolf, a cry that he says
stirred the emotions of every living thing that heard it—the deer and
the pine, the coyote, the rancher, and the hunter; perhaps, he adds,
many a dead thing as well. "Only the mountain," he writes, "has lived
long enough to listen objectively to the howl of a wolf."

In his youth Leopold never passed up a chance to kill a wolf. Once
when he and some friends were eating lunch on a high rimrock, they
spotted a female wolf and her pups playing below. In a second the men
were firing into the pack. "When our rifles were empty, the old wolf
was down, and a pup was dragging a leg into impassable slide-rocks."

> We reached the old wolf in time to watch a fierce green fire dying in her
> eyes. I realized then, and have known ever since, that there was some-
> thing new to me in those eyes—something known only to her and to the
> mountain. I was young then, and full of trigger-itch; I thought that be-

cause fewer wolves meant more deer, that no wolves would mean hunters' paradise. But after seeing the green fire die, I sensed that neither the wolf nor the mountain agreed with such a view.

The death of fire in the wolf's eyes was the birth of fire in Leopold, a fire to hear a wolf in a way that does not come naturally to living things: not with the apprehension of the deer, the hatred of the rancher, or the feverishness of the hunter, but with the time-honored objectivity of a mountain. An objectivity that, as I see it, is a silence that is endless and respectful and soul-full, a deep-space silence that signifies nothing more troublesome than a willing acceptance of the universe. The baby carriage is not empty; it contains us all. Leopold ends by suggesting that it is the mountain's objectivity that is behind Thoreau's observation, "In Wildness is the preservation of the World." "Perhaps," he writes, "this is the hidden meaning in the howl of the wolf, long known among mountains, but seldom perceived among men."

In the star-studded night on my sloping field of snow, my search for Lefty became a search for the mountain itself.

Not even a night out without a sleeping bag could discourage the remarkable Bert Hegewa. In the morning he crawled out from under his spruce, shook himself off, and booby-trapped the wolf trail.

The first day he caught a coyote. When he inspected the area the following morning he discovered fresh wolf prints fifty feet from the main runway. The pack had come through, all right, but at the last moment had veered to avoid the coyote, which had come through first.

Hegewa booby-trapped the detour. That night the pack returned and again took the cutoff. Running in the lead, Lefty leapt a branch that Hegewa had placed strategically in the trail. When the wolf came down, he landed in not one but two of Hegewa's traps.

The traps were not staked to the ground, so Lefty could still travel, but only with difficulty. Each trap weighed more than five pounds; moreover, heavy drag hooks raked along behind them as the wolf moved, impeding his progress and leaving deep furrows in the snow to mark his route. Somewhere one of the hooks jammed in an obstruction in the path. As Hegewa discovered later, the wolf pulled with such power that he straightened the drag hook and broke free. When a second hook caught in a clump of sagebrush, however, Lefty hadn't the strength to pull out. It was there that Hegewa and the cowboy found him in the morning.

Stanley Young describes the wolf as huge, bedraggled, red-eyed, and enraged. The cowboy roped him around the neck and pulled tight, stretching the animal away from the captured drag hook. Hegewa cut a branch from an aspen tree and laid it over Lefty's shoulders, pinning the wolf to the ground. With the animal battling beneath him, he eased himself out onto the branch, one knee on Lefty's abdomen, the other on his neck. Gingerly he slipped a noose over the wildly snapping jaws and clamped them shut. Then he hog-tied the animal so that it was unable to move.

There was no honor to a fallen leader in what came next. Hegewa wrapped a collar around Lefty's neck, chained him to a stake, and surrounded him with traps. Then he and the cowboy returned to the cabin, leaving the wolf behind as live bait for the other members of the pack.

That night and for several nights afterward, the pack returned. Three more wolves fell into Hegewa's traps. The others, if there were others, abandoned the mountain. Ranchers reported that the wolf tracks to be seen on Castle Peak grew fainter over the next few months and disappeared with the first spring rains. Fresh tracks were never seen again.

Young scrupulously avoids mentioning the actual death of Lefty. We learn only that Hegewa brought in a bottle of the wolf's scent, his pelt, and his head, the latter to be mounted as a trophy, open-jawed and snarling. The carcass Hegewa left on the mountain for scavengers.

A few weeks after Hegewa departed, local stockmen wrote to the Biological Survey in Denver thanking the agency for the hunter's services:

It is a big relief to us to know that "Old Lefty" is a thing of the past—for his track on the range meant he was back and on the job of cattle killing once again. We breathe a sigh of keen satisfaction, and fully realize the capture of "Old Lefty" was truly a job for you Government men who study out these things and apply methods no ordinary amateur can touch.

A few scattered pockets of resistance remained in the far corners of the state. Conflicting reports put the date of the final eradication of wolves from Colorado at 1935 and 1941. A 1938 report states that two wolves were seen that year in Colorado's national forests. A Monte Vista taxidermist claimed that a wolf was killed in Conejos County in 1943. In 1967 two old and no doubt nostalgia-drunk bounty hunters reported that they saw a wolf near Parlin, but no one believed them.

Species	*Last Seen*
Kenai Peninsula Wolf	1910
Newfoundland Wolf	1911
Banks Island Wolf	1920
Florida Red Wolf	1925
Great Plains Wolf	1926
Mogollon Mountains Wolf	1934
Cascade Mountains Wolf	1940
Northern Rocky Mountains Wolf	1941
Texas Gray Wolf	1942
Texas Red Wolf	1970
Southern Rocky Mountains Wolf	1970

Five to six thousand wolves remain today in Alaska, where they are said to be in no danger of extinction. The Alaska Department of Fish and Game reports that hunters killed 844 wolves in the state in 1989. In the contiguous United States, wild wolves survive only near the Canadian border—about a thousand in northern Minnesota, scattered groups of a dozen or two at a handful of other locations. Recently, red wolves have been reintroduced on an experimental basis into a federal wildlife refuge in North Carolina. And in New Mexico, the four-thousand-square-mile White Sands Missile Range has been proposed as a site for reintroduction of the Mexican wolf, a species probably extinct in the wild. Thirty of the animals have been bred in captivity in zoos in Albuquerque, Tucson, and St. Louis. But plans to release them onto White Sands have been stalled for several years and perhaps permanently, due to opposition from the army, which operates the range, and from ranchers beyond its borders.

> A photograph of jaguars
> An elk head on a wall
> A monument to petrels
> Skins of mink and fox
> Petroglyphs of bison
> Memories of cranes
> Pigeons in museums
> Deer tracks in the snow
> Weathervanes of roosters
> Clouds resembling horses
> Condors in pale moonlight
> A pack of stars called Lupus

I never found Old Lefty. The howl I heard toward sunset was an auditory illusion, a symptom of the high mountain madness that sometimes afflicts the lonely and the hopeful. What I did find, as I settled to my observation post among the sage and the night wore on and the cold air pressed in around me, was a flawless spinning of the gears, of the night and the cold, of the earth, the sage, the snow, the air, the mountain, and the star-jammed sky—a reliable clockwork that, for a few moments at least, seemed to number me among its busily twirling wheels.

I had been monitoring the flashing lights of Orion, that irrepressible peacock, when it came to me that I wanted to feel the cold, really feel it, as I had never felt it before. Without further thought I peeled off my mittens, my wool cap, and my coat, and tossed them down at my side. Then I stood as calmly as I could (I froze, we might say) and waited. I was sure that something curious was going to happen.

The night air coiled around me, tightened its grip, and penetrated my skin, and the warmth of my body drained away. But, strangely, I felt no discomfort, no urge to shiver or tighten down on my muscles. I stood tranquilly, my arms at my sides, my face turned toward the sky. The cold swelled within me. I closed my eyes and listened. Not a sound broke the icebound calm, not an atom danced in the rock-still air. I was afloat in the deepest silence I had ever known, a silence black and bottomless and perfect. It evoked in me a feeling that was unfamiliar and gratifying, a sense that I had discovered something I had fervently believed in but, until that moment, had never experienced as truth.

Soon the feeling passed and the quiet lifted, and I began to shiver violently. I opened my eyes and knelt to retrieve my wrappings. Quickly I zipped up my coat, pulled on my mittens, and tugged my cap down over my ears.

It was late. I had a long hike ahead of me to reach my car, and it was time to get moving.

I looked east, where the tip of the crescent moon was a dot of light on the horizon. The sky was clear and would soon be bright; the air was calm. It was a good night to travel a mountain.

I took my pack in my hand and started down the slope. After a few steps I stopped. Something seemed wrong. I could feel the black hulk of Castle Peak behind me, and, higher up, the topmost rocks perched in the distant sky.

I hesitated only a moment. Then I turned, pulled my pack over my shoulders, and headed for the top of the mountain.

This one's for Lefty.

Socrates
in the
Catskills

SOCRATES: *But by the by, Phaedrus, was not
this the tree to which you were leading me?*
PHAEDRUS: *The very one.*
SOCRATES: *Well, really, this is a glorious resting
place.*

PLATO, *Phaedrus*

I

September has arrived, the polished, apple-bright mornings of Indian summer gleam with their delectable urgency, and the nation has declared war, yet again, on the deplorable state of education in America. That the stirring call to arms is in fact an annual event as dependable as the harvest moon and nearly as ancient is a bit of trivia not widely known, but it is true; I have the newspaper clippings to prove it. We declare war in September when the children return to school, then

abandon the fight before the roll is called. It is as though the mere statement of purpose alone were sufficient to secure victory. In October
those of us still itching for a scrap solemnly take up arms against some
other foe—drugs, cancer, pornography, inflation, rock lyrics, drunk
drivers, Saturday morning television commercials. And so on until
bright September returns and we can begin again at the top of the list.
So crowded is the calendar that we run the risk of confusing one enemy
with the next or forgetting an old adversary altogether, and when we
meet again we may think we are squaring off for the first time. The blur-
ring of the battle lines has a richly soothing effect, permitting us the de-
lusion that strategies which fizzled in the past will somehow hit home
this time around. I think, too, it accounts for the dizzying optimism
that accompanied the most celebrated resumption of hostilities in recent years, in September 1989, when President Bush and the nation's
governors put their heads together for a two-day "education summit"
in Charlottesville, Virginia, to map out a plan for defeating the black-
bearded guerrillas of ignorance once and for all.

I confess to rather unpatriotic trepidations about whether this war
would end any more triumphantly than the rest. Nevertheless, because my stake in the outcome was enormous, I dutifully hoisted my
somewhat tattered edition of Old Glory and cheered lustily for the governors in their bunker. My involvement in this business was almost too
dreadful to admit to. Through the stormy decade leading up to the year
1975 I taught high school mathematics in New York City. In later years
I edited secondary school math textbooks for one of the dwindling
number of educational publishers that still behaved as if there were
hope, and then went on to write a few texts of my own, some of which
even now languish in the nation's classrooms.

Above all, I was now happily awaiting the birth of my first child,
and, nature having worked her peculiar magic, I had my eye squarely
on the future. Without much difficulty I could imagine my still imag-
inary son or daughter cowering under a desk in a smoke-blackened

school somewhere, while outside the dreaded guerrillas hurled spears and hand grenades at the front door. Meanwhile, in a storeroom at the back of the school, several cartons of my textbooks crackled in flames.

Pessimistic, yes, but desperate; without a moment of hesitation I threw in my lot with the governors, at the same time offering up a fervent prayer that they bomb those pesky mudboots back into the Stone Age.

Alas, my doubts proved prophetic. At the conclusion of the conference, just before the president and his guests ducked into their creamy limousines and sped away, they issued a statement of intent that only rehashed an old and tired litany of goals: improve test scores, reduce dropout rates, upgrade work skills, prepare students to compete more effectively with their counterparts in Europe and the Far East. Most of the familiar goals seemed to miss the point entirely, but no matter; even had they hit the mark the governors had little to say about how to achieve them. Worse, they said nothing at all about Socrates.

I mention Socrates, that lovable, bald-headed, pot-bellied old gadfly, because it seems to me that any blueprint for educational reform that fails to take him as its inspiration is doomed from the start. If we do not think of Socrates as an educator or the dialogues Plato so exquisitely rendered for us as lessons, that is because we have drifted so far from the examples those men set us. Socrates, you'll recall, ran his school, such as it was, wherever he happened to be when it was time for class to begin; that is, anywhere at any time. One day it was a portico near the Acropolis, the next the refreshing shade of a plane tree on the banks of the Ilissus. Having chosen his post, he engaged anyone who happened along in a lively inquiry into the nature of truth, virtue, beauty, wisdom, or some other completely useless topic, which the two then proceeded to drive completely into the ground. Education, you might guess, was not the rueful, sackcloth-and-ashes business it has become today. The participants in these colloquies actually seem to enjoy themselves, a variation on the current mode the governors in Charlottesville would doubtless have found worrisome. As for the impracticality of his speculations, Socrates wore it as something of a badge of honor. He had nothing but harsh words for the Sophists, those itinerant teachers who instructed the rising middle class of Athens in the practical skills they would need to achieve success in their dog-eat-dog metropolis.

It was trivial, this spat with the Sophists, but in it we hear for the first time the distant rumblings of the great conflict between generalist and specialist which would soon erupt and quickly deteriorate into a bitter separation, where it remains to this day. A mathematics teacher might fix the date of the breakup as 212 B.C., some two centuries after the death of Socrates, when the Roman army overran Syracuse. As the victors poured through the gates of the city, a Roman soldier came upon the great Archimedes, who was lost in contemplation of a geometrical figure he had scratched in the sand. The soldier struck him dead. To Alfred North Whitehead this act symbolized "a world change of the first magnitude. The Romans were a great race," he conceded, scarcely concealing his rage, "but they were cursed by the sterility which waits upon practicality. They were not dreamers enough to arrive at new points of view."

In forswearing practicality Socrates was being a bit ingenuous, for surely he must have recognized that the clear and critical thinking and speaking skills his method encouraged were eminently practical; a graduate of a conversation with Socrates was wonderfully prepared to succeed in Athens, much as a student today who is able to think, speak, and write clearly and critically is prepared to succeed in his or her chosen field—and, incidentally, to meet, rather spectacularly I should guess, the goals of the Charlottesville manifesto. It was precisely Socrates' skill as a logician and a rhetorician, I think, that drew others to him, since only mastery of one's subject matter can attract students to a teacher.

Still, he would have declined the compliment and insisted in one of his favorite metaphors that he was only a poor midwife helping students bring thoughts to life. This idea that thoughts are eternal and through devout inquiry we can discover them is central to his and to Plato's philosophy, and strikingly similar to the beliefs of the followers of a variety of traditions—Buddhists, for example, who hold that our original nature was that of the enlightened Buddha and that we have only forgotten it, or the Transcendentalists of our own nineteenth century, who among the rocks of New England sought universal truths, hidden there—divine Easter eggs—to be turned up by the diligent seeker.

And my own tradition, that of the mountain climber, which declares that learning to climb is simply a matter of remembering what one could do naturally as a child, or before. Indeed, the effort of bringing a thought to life, as Socrates would have it, is not altogether unlike the effort of climbing a mountain. Look: our heroes come together in the shade of a spreading plane tree and there share a pleasantry or two, perhaps a cup of tea. No doubt uneasy at the prospect before them, they gear up dilatorily, probe the subject gingerly and without resolve. Suddenly, an opening laid bare, they take the irreversible step, commit themselves fully to the struggle. Progress now is erratic. At first they move smoothly, but soon they are blundering up blind alleys or wandering off in odd directions, there to reap great or grievous rewards. They move as a team but as individuals too, challenging, encouraging, criticizing, stumbling, doubting, strutting their stuff. They proceed with no firm sense of where they are going, only an unshakable conviction, rooted in their bones, that it is upward. They work out a giddy, scary, thoroughly engrossing route among the pitfalls—what a climber would call a first ascent except that, for Socrates, at least, the summit is rarely reached. For him as for the mountaineer, it is the climb that counts, and many of his explorations dissipate into thin air, lacking even a summing up. For truly, there are few answers in Socrates.

Happily, however, the search can easily be directed toward practicable ends should the teacher so desire. In the *Meno*, Plato gives us an example of one such excursion, as Socrates leads a slave boy through a rather demanding argument in mathematics:

SOCRATES: Then the line which forms the side of eight feet ought to be more than this line of two feet, and less than the other of four feet?

BOY: It ought.

SOCRATES: Try and see if you can tell me how much it will be.

BOY: Three feet.

SOCRATES: Then if we add a half to this line of two, that will be the line of three. Here are two and there is one; and on the other side, here are two also and there is one: and that makes the figure of which you speak?

BOY: Yes.

SOCRATES: But if there are three feet this way and three feet that way, the whole space will be three feet times three feet?

BOY: That is evident.

The Charlottesville conferees might have enjoyed a performance of the entire dialogue—perhaps preceded by ouzo and belly dancers—especially the thrilling climax, in which the slave boy discovers (*remembers*, Socrates reminds us) that a square erected on the diagonal of a given square will have an area twice that of the first. Had the stunning dénouement seemed a trifle unbelievable (the slave boy was not previously on an academic track), the audience might still have applauded these incidental lessons from the show, lessons apparent in all of Socrates: small classes, an excellent student-teacher ratio, individualized instruction, a safe environment for learning, no class interruptions, and no drugs. (Elsewhere, hemlock is mentioned, but it was reserved for the teacher. Among the charges brought against Socrates, charges which ultimately cost him his life, was that of corrupting the youth of Athens; that is, encouraging them to question *everything*, including the established values of the city. It was a charge to which I should think any teacher would be happy to answer.)

Stripped of the rhetorical fireworks that usually capture our attention, what the Socratic model provides and what is sorely missing from our annual prescriptions for educational reform is a trenchant reminder that education is *precisely* a conversation between two people, teacher and student, who have agreed to embark on an adventure together. It is a joining of two minds, not twenty or thirty, not one mind and a computer, in a quest for truth, an endeavor as necessary to life as laughter and as love. A teacher is what Socrates was, an ardent, caring, learned, occasionally floundering guide led by his inner light. We must not suppose that he or she is perfect; today we shudder at Socrates' authoritarian views, his support for slavery, his belief in an aristocracy of power. It is not the purpose of the quest to lead the student to the teacher's truth; rather, the two of them should aspire to a greater truth. Having made their compact, they step into the unknown together, intrepid mountaineers, each urging the other to a higher plane.

Every teacher knows those magical moments when the plan for the day is tossed aside and an inexplicable energy seizes the classroom, and students and teacher alike are propelled at breathtaking speed, infusing one another with what Alfred Adler has described as "a spirit of disciplined search for adventures of the intellect." In these priceless moments we discover a second ingredient that is missing from our annual September prescriptions, and that is passion, the lifeblood of the age of first love and rap and rock 'n' roll, the age when the heart discovers its song and its searchless dimensions. A teenager cannot so much as answer a phone without it. The teacher who lacks it is lost.

We all remember the one who had it; it is the reason we remember. In my public high school in Titusville, Pennsylvania, it was Arnold Jeschke, a tall, sandy-haired, slightly mysterious man whose most intriguing feature was a nearly imperceptible, close-lipped smile; ambiguous, yes, but reassuring too, a winsome vote for ambiguity, the first we his students had ever encountered. Arnold Jeschke conducted English class the way Bernstein conducted Bernstein—with panache, with his whole body and soul, with the preposterous conviction that what he was communicating was not only himself but all of creation too, and that it had the supreme and radical importance of life and death. Striding up and down the aisles, thundering, imploring—a word here, a frown, a gentle supplication: he wanted *so much*! He taught students at all levels, respected the unique and precious gift of each, and expected perfection from all. We memorized passages from Milton, Gray, and Keats because if we did not, his despair would destroy us. A gallant soul once screwed up his courage to ask: "When will we be finished with Shakespeare?"

It was a set-up a teacher might wait a lifetime for.

"NEVER!" cried Arnold Jeschke. As the word burst from his lips he slammed his fist onto his desk, raising the entire class as one from our seats. Yet by the familiar twinkle in his eyes we understood that the agony was not to be ours alone, that this impossible man would suffer Shakespeare with us through the ages.

What I mean to say is this: Let us have *teachers*, impassioned teachers, starry-eyed teachers, bold, dashing teachers, Marco Polos of science, literature, history, language, and social studies. And this: classes of twelve or fourteen, no more, for as Socrates has taught us, each student must hold a conversation with the teacher every day. To pay for this grand Socratic revolution, let us confiscate the billions currently earmarked for building improvements (we shall meet in the parking lot, thank you), high-tech gadgetry (computers, television sets, and other paraphernalia are merely diversionary; anyway, schools are for people), self-justifying administrators (mostly former teachers; why did they leave?), and new textbooks (which despite improved packaging contain essentially the same unimproved wisdom as the old); and let us use it to buy teachers. Our dreams will be realized overnight. Test scores will skyrocket. Employers will trample one another to hire our graduates. The Germans and the Japanese will quiver in their boots.

The school board, of course, will denounce me as a fantasist and sputter that Socrates is dead, Arnold Jeschke retired, and the world a very dark place. Nonsense. The schools are full of teachers such as I have described, for I have described precisely the kind of person who

sets out to be a teacher. Today they do not loll by the Ilissus chattering
with their students. Instead they take roll (in some classes the major ac-
complishment of the day), write lesson plans, attend meetings, com-
pile endless administrative reports, quiet their understandably furious
classes in order to listen to mindless announcements over abhorrent
public address systems. *Liberate these divine creatures!* Give them per-
mission to teach.

As for students: September hysterics to the contrary, the schools are
brimming with fine young men and women who are avid to converse
with their teachers in sublime peace, who would rather love learning
than drugs, and who even today are eager to burn a portion of their
boundless energy chasing after those storied adventures of the intellect. In classes of forty or thirty or even twenty, they haven't a chance; a
good-sized plane tree, by my measurement, holds about a dozen.
There in the refreshing shade, protected from the enervating rays of the
sun, they can taste what mountaineers enjoy each step of the journey
to the summit, what George Pólya called "the triumph of discovery."
Pólya, one of the twentieth century's foremost mathematicians and
perhaps our leading investigator into the mechanics of everyday
problem-solving, wrote knowingly of the gratification of discovery. He
held out this genial reward not just to the Watsons, Cricks, and Pólyas
of the world, but to all of us. Take a challenge to the curiosity, exercise
a little creativity or inventiveness, cook up a personal solution, and
there it is—a high worthy of Newton. I don't know if Pólya discussed
endorphins, but it seems clear now that the release of these delicious
chemicals into the brain is responsible for the exhilaration we feel as we
solve a crossword puzzle or put together a strategy for defeating the
competition or work our way through a difficult argument by Socrates.
They are habit-forming, these endorphins; the brain that gobbles them
too young or too often can become addicted for a lifetime.

Now then, boys and girls, what I have here is a lovely new drug. Just
say yes.

II

The teacher who follows too closely in the footsteps of Socrates had best beware, for he and his students may soon be climbing mountains together. At Riverdale Country School, a private school in the high Republican district of the Bronx, I became friends with Peter Owens and Leon Bills, fellow faculty members who on winter weekends went off, in defiance of prudence, to snowshoe in the Catskills. Sometimes they dragged students and other gullibles along, and one Friday in February they invited me, a new member of the faculty, to join them the following day.

I knew nothing about snowshoeing, and nothing that was true about the Catskills. To me as, I suspect, to most residents of New York City, the word *Catskills* brought to mind the fabled resorts—Grossingers, the Concord, and the rest—that abutted the foothills a few miles south of the mountains proper. When I thought of the Catskills I thought of lawn chairs and martinis and slightly weatherbeaten comedians cracking jokes about their mothers-in-law. Any suggestion of hiking, let alone snowshoeing, in the Catskills was likely to bring a chuckle. What—out behind the tennis courts?

How often, in how many ways do the mountains surprise us. From afar the climber spies a polished wall thrusting skyward and his blood runs cold; as he continues his approach he sees the wall lean back and the menacing surface condense into funky streets and alleys, as an alluring route to the summit opens up. So step back, gaze higher . . . up there above the pool and the tennis courts, where the horizon is restless and the sky an implausible blue. Turn away from the main road and follow the unmarked lane that winds curiously upward beside the creek and into the misty trees. Travel slowly and with an open heart, as though even today, in our winter of relentless explication, there are mysteries yet to be explained . . .

"You know the Cattskills, lad; for you must have seen them on your left, as you followed the river up from York, looking as blue as a piece of clear sky, and holding the clouds on their tops, as the smoke curls over the head of an Indian chief at the council fire. Well, there's the High-peak, and the Round-top which lay back like a father and mother among their children, seeing they are far above all the other hills. But the place I mean is next to the river, where one of the ridges juts out a little from the rest, and where the rocks fall, for the best part of a thousand feet, so much up and down, that a man standing on their edges is fool enough to think he can jump from top to bottom."

"What see you when you get there?" asked Edwards.

"Creation," said Natty, dropping the end of his rod into the water, and sweeping one hand around him in a circle: "all creation, lad."

Natty, our beloved Leatherstocking, here starring in James Fenimore Cooper's *The Pioneers*. Before the Cascades and the High Sierra lifted out of the West to stagger our imaginations, before the great Rockies rose up to trouble the emigrant's sleep; even before New Hampshire's gentle White Mountains laid claim to the title of Alps of America, the Catskills stole the nation's breath away, made the pulse race with that captivating fever of desire and fear that has characterized the human response to mountains since the beginning. The Catskills, dark and impenetrable, steep, tightly packed mountains cloaked in deep forests of spruce and balsam fir. At the start of the nineteenth century few of our compatriots had an inkling of what was going on in there. When Washington Irving lost his Rip van Winkle in the Catskills for twenty years, his readers believed him. Irving was only building on a well-established tradition, for Catskill lore abounded in tales that bespoke remoteness and mystery—witches, lost treasure, strange creatures like the bears whose hind legs measured three feet longer than their front. Thus equipped, these uneven beasts could race up the steep mountainsides like jackrabbits. (How they descended without snowballing head over heels down the mountain, no one ever explained.)

Even today an exciting sense of wildness pervades the region. Unlike the gemlike villages of many of the world's mountainous areas, Catskill settlements have never quite overcome their surroundings. They're pale, sober, hardscrabble places, birch seedlings struggling in the hollows. Between them, gnarly roads follow the crazy will of the wild. In this thousand-square-mile region between Albany and New York City, most of it in the state-administered Catskill Forest Preserve, thirty-four peaks rise to a height of more than 3,500 feet. A Coloradan accustomed to fourteen-thousand-footers might not be impressed, but these are real mountains, as Natty tried to tell us. If you go, hang on to your hat. I discovered this quickly in the company of my friends that Saturday morning in February: moments after exiting the car and strapping on the fateful snowshoes, my fingers went numb and my resolve vanished without a trace. A bitter wind swept down on us from high on Peekamoose Mountain. I pounded my hands together, massaged my fingers furiously inside my mittens. It was evident to all that the mountain was firmly in control of the morning. Impatient to get moving (better foolishly than not at all), we shouldered our packs and tramped off into the woods.

What a malfunction snowshoeing seemed, the feet so gawky and self-conscious, yet somehow by their very gracelessness empowered to tread the feathery snow. Unlike skiing, which I knew well, snowshoeing was bumpy and rambling, a buckboard ride to your fancy turboglide. I loved it. We bounded up the mountainside like spaniels, scooted between narrowly spaced hemlocks as no skier ever could. Here and there we broke out into pocket-size meadows, alluring winter gardens rolling in hip-smooth drifts of snow. We dashed merrily across, possessed by the day. My chest heaved; I felt gorgeously alive. There was no trail. Like Tenzing and Hillary, we created our own. Alarums and diversions occurred. Several times we got lost. Often I fell in the snow. We never found the top of the mountain. Best of all, Leon's nose froze. In scant seconds what had been a ruddy, excellent nose turned the density of cast iron and the color of vanilla ice cream.

All of this seemed superbly educational. I went along on three or four such expeditions and began to agree with my friends that there might be something here for students to learn. It couldn't be taught directly, that was clear; I wasn't even sure what it was. But more and more I felt I had found something in the Catskills that I needed to share. A young person would have to be brought here as he or she might be brought to Faulkner or Stravinsky, and then encouraged to trudge unsteadily upward through the thick and entrancing woods. I made up my mind that one day I would take kids to the mountains and that there, with Thoreau, we would see if we could not learn what the woods had to teach.

My first opportunity came in 1972 at New York City's Collegiate School, where I put in my final three years in the classroom. Founded in 1628, Collegiate is the oldest independent school in the country. I didn't know it at the time, but I see now that it is also one of America's premier neo-Socratic academies. At Collegiate we didn't meet under the plane trees, but we did hold classes in an ancient building on the Upper West Side just off Broadway which, when the humidity was high and the smell of old wood just right, seemed a prime site for an archeological dig; not Athenian, perhaps, but close enough that we could easily overlook the difference. Unlike Socrates, who refused compensation for his services, we teachers were paid, but again the difference was marginal. That first year I earned about seven thousand dollars. The headmaster then as now was Richard Barter, an amiable and unassuming man who, like Agathon, had the wit to recognize that although the party was held at his house, so to speak, he was just another guest at the symposium. There were two or three other administrators, all similarly enlightened. The prevailing view at Collegiate seemed to be that education is a folding together of teacher and student and that, like an angel food cake, it must be done slowly and quietly, and without jiggling. Thus we were spared announcement marathons, pep rallies, mindless interruptions, ten o'clock surprises. There were no unscheduled assemblies, no lesson plans to prepare, no administrative papers to push. From above came this simple directive: take this chalk and this handful of boys (for Collegiate was an all-boys school), close the door, and see what happens. What happened was that when the door opened and the boys came out, they achieved wonderful College Board scores, attended fine colleges, and secured excellent jobs. Even better, they were educated. The governors in Charlottesville would have been impressed.

Because the school was small, about forty students per grade, only three other teachers shared Middle and Upper School math classes with me. The chair of the math department was Elaine Genkins, a brilliant and caring teacher, a cornerstone to build a school around. She and I handled the Upper School, Linda Villari and Dave Hertz the Middle School. Dave and I joined the faculty the same year and quickly discovered a mutual fondness for pipe-smoking. We became fast friends. Between classes we rushed to the math office and hurriedly lit up (this was in the quaint era before non-smokers' lib), rapidly filling the room with gray clouds stout with the fragrances of Arabia and Tidore. It is a wonder the fire department was never called. The sense of the exotic was heightened because the math office, like the school and the faculty, was minuscule—a dark, cramped, low-ceilinged room which, besides billowing in smoke most of the time, hissed perpetually with the stridor of a recalcitrant steam radiator. The math office at Collegiate School reminded me of the boiler room on a tramp steamer bound for Karachi.

In theory, this quirky domicile was the math faculty's haven of rest and recuperation. But adventures are continuous and Socrates taught from dawn to dusk. I cannot recall a moment in three years when our haven was not jammed to the ceiling with jabbering kids. (But is there ever escape for a teacher? After school I sometimes walked home with one or two of my students, in the evening and on weekends I put in long hours at the kitchen table correcting papers, and sometimes late at night I answered the phone and heard a sad or weary or frightened voice faltering at the other end of the line: "Mr. Reid . . . ?" Surely it is true, as Shaw's Henry Higgins observed, that teaching would be impossible unless students were sacred.)

Not long after arriving at Collegiate I began leading weekend hikes in the Catskills, thereby fulfilling the vow I had made a few years earlier. Once or twice a month on Saturdays bright with sunshine or blustery with snow, ten or twelve of us ventured two hours north to school in the mountains where Leatherstocking had promised we might see all of creation. I was not alone at the helm of these expeditions. Dave Hertz became my constant companion on the trail. Sometimes headmaster Dick Barter joined us, thereby neatly obliterating the mistaken class distinctions that sometimes divide faculty from administration. In two years we climbed several dozen of the highest peaks in the Catskills, some of them two or three times, and from high up on airy promontories and deep down in the rude underbrush studied a goodly portion of downstate New York. About a quarter of the student body came along at one time or another, voluntary truth-seekers all. They came, a few explained to me later, because it seemed wayward to do so. Waywardness, I have neglected to mention, was part of the curriculum at Collegiate School.

One Friday afternoon, weary, of course, but cheered by the prospect of a tramp in the mountains less than twenty-four hours away, I announced to my geometry class, completely to my surprise, that we would spend the remainder of the period playing the game of Chester. We were gathered in one of Collegiate's wonderfully peculiar classrooms (ceiling slanting roguishly from front to back, windows the size of portholes) and I had never before heard of the game of Chester.

But teaching is something like jazz, and it is well to have an agile set of chops. "The object," I explained, hurriedly seeking one, "is to figure out ten ways to use the word *Chester* in a sentence." I searched for a moment and then I said, "I keep my socks in a Chester drawers," getting the contestants started with the only way I knew to use the word *Chester* in a sentence. They accepted all of this as though it were important, which it was.

"My uncle lives in West Chester County," offered one, the kid who jumps first off the bridge. He had not raised his hand, nor had Socrates' student in the *Meno*.

I smiled.

Another: "Chester Arthur was once a president, I think. Or Arthur Chester."

"Yes, well . . . Anyone else?"

"Chester, the guy who limps on 'Gunsmoke.' "

Not a sentence, but never mind. Six to go, and please—a little off-road rattle-and-roll. "Chestern left, you can't miss it," I said, indicating the direction, and off we went.

"Is this in Chester are you serious?"

"I hate getting hit in the Chester stomach."

"Chester-minate this nonsense at once!"

"I'll have Chester-key and stuffing, thank you."

A pause and then, from Stewart Gross, whose triumphant countenance I can still call to mind after fifteen years: "Bobby Fischer won the Chester-nament."

I recall a standing ovation. Outside the window, on tumbledown 77th Street, on skulking, menacing Broadway, another world spun crazily off-course. In this world, where mastery and passion are accorded the highest honors, you will learn to find peace and beauty in the world beyond. This is job training, then, just as you have been told. Your job is to learn to use your head and your heart. On an earlier watch I drove a station wagon to Riverdale Country School each morning, first stopping to pick up five or six young passengers at their townhouses on New York's affluent Upper East Side. One morning, instead of turning onto the East River Drive after a uniformed doorman had helped the last of my charges into the car, we headed north, across the forbidden border at 96th Street, up Madison to 125th, up Lenox Avenue and St. Nicholas—north through the streets of Harlem. It was widely advised that this was a journey to take on the fly, so grievous were the supposed consequences of a misstep. But we did not hurry, we dawdled that April morning in 1968, touring back and forth from one street to the next in our indomitable Riverdale wagon, past smoking buildings and looted store windows, past burning trash baskets and crowds of vacant-eyed people standing broken on the broken sidewalks of Harlem. And as we toured we talked, we practiced our heads and our hearts, for Martin Luther King was dead that morning in Memphis, and we had mountains and mountains to learn. It was my finest moment as a teacher, I think, so boldly risking the hemlock.

III

Saturday. What does Socrates remember about preparations for class? The abomination of an alarm clock crying in the night. The prancing of bare feet on arctic bathroom tile. The sheer horror of scrambled eggs at five o'clock in the morning. A surreal walk through the sulfurous West Side dawn, the metallic undersong of the city. An arm-slapping, breath-snapping, Siberian sunup in February, and twelve kids with dazed Saturday-morning eyes. (For a day of rock climbing in the Shawangunks two hours north of the city, I once hopped a subway at dawn to meet a friend with a car at the end of the line. My climbing hardware I had hidden deftly enough in my rucksack, but the bulky climbing rope I was forced to wear over my shoulder like a ridiculous epaulet. As I stepped onto the subway at 96th and Broadway, a young woman glanced up from her newspaper and spotted me. "Whataya gonna do, Mister?" she called to me in a disapproving voice. "Hang yourself?") Dave takes six kids, I do the same, and we're off, down 72nd Street to the West Side Highway, to the room with the slanted roof.

The energy level in the car is nuclear. The radio blares rock 'n' roll, kids croon goofily like underage saloon singers. They have whimsical, inscrutable nicknames. Tim is Mort. Michael is Doc. Hank is Johnson. No one can explain why; the question is meaningless. Stewart is Sito, the lost Socratic dialogue. Most mysterious of all is Jim, who has somehow become Eddie. Were he Slug or Arf we might at least appreciate the consistency. But Eddie?

As the city winks out in the rearview mirror, the magic essence of the morning sweeps in over fields of old corn. Pointy-beaked snowflakes swoop past us like swallows; white drifts lap higher on the legs of cigarette and motor oil ads. Altitude-sick, I acclaim the first hulking shadows on the horizon. To identify, to surrender: head and heart, mind and spirit, the old formulation. The union of these two indispensable tools the Greeks called perfect *aretē*; attaining it, they believed, secured a home for you on Olympus. Their symbol for the impossible quest: the mountain climb.

At Phoenicia (yes, that is the name) we converge on Peruski's for doughnuts, gas, and a little misadventure. In the parking lot Dave and I warm a fender apiece and sip steaming French roast from plastic Thermos cups. Inside a dozen kids overwhelm poor Peruski. Are there enough doughnuts in all of Ulster County for these ravenous urchins? I check the topo map, explain to anyone who asks what I know, which isn't much. Just above the phone lines the sun is white leather, a mean slider, low and away. Icing up, we jog absurdly in place. The serrated air goes down like moonshine.

"LET'S GET OUTA HERE!"

The road is not yet plowed, so we follow the tracks of an unknown benefactor who has kindly opened the way. Chains slapping the hard snow beneath us, we cross the border, check our passports, move deeper into Kashmir. My passengers are quiet, restless, bemused by the labyrinth of possibilities. Peering out the windows so hopefully (there to freeze indelibly in my memory), they are haunting expressions of the infinite beauty of kids. The way narrows; the snow slants harder from the west. Slim mint and wintergreen trees bend over the road and touch their tips in the sky. Rounding a corner, I spot a clearing with space for two. Pumping my brakes gently I slip quietly into my stall.

I order my passengers to bundle up (as if they need to be told: it is 5° outside). A sharp wind badgers us through the hemlock. They must wonder how we are going to turn this to our advantage; certainly I do. On hands and knees I crawl from foot to foot checking snowshoe straps. "They shouldn't be too tight," I wheeze. "They'll cut off your circulation and you'll get frostbite."

They laugh. What's frostbite to a teenager!

"They shouldn't be too loose either."

"Thanks, Bob."

"I'm just telling you."

(Sometimes I worried that they all would die. Back in the city I would have to phone their parents with the bad news. How do you explain to a mother that you have just marched her child off a cliff?)

As we enter the woods an inexpressible contentment seizes me, a sense of utter engagement with the world. They feel it, too; it carries them in a surge of laughter and excitement pell-mell into the trees, a snowstorm of bodies, explosive and reckless. A forest can do that to you. The blast detonates a hail of sparrows in the trees above us. In a panic Dave and I round up the insurgents and lay down the law: I'll go first, he'll go last to protect the rear flank. The rest of you: in between! It's a fine plan, one that lasts about as long as it takes to announce it. For the rest of the day the threat of mutiny will be ever-present. And why not: they all believe I can be out-talked in the dialogue.

As we go higher, deeper into the trees, we turn inward, slowly warming to the grandeur of the mountain. The path slants more steeply now, the gospel of gravity is a sweet jab in the thighs. I check the compass, search trailside for markers and tree blazes. We call a halt and check our bones for a reading. I announce my opinion: This way. Dave says: That. Like a chessboard knight we zigzag up the mountain, our direction finder a folksy muddle of science and witchcraft. Someone has demonstrated that by pooling their completely untutored guesses, a group of ten or twelve can average out a rock-solid truth. This, then, is how we approach *aretē*: we average our way to the top of the mountain.

The curious footwear opens the way. In a burst of pride I explain the amazing principle of the snowshoe: Go where you will, truth-seeker; if you get in a pickle, just turn around and follow your tracks home. The others shout at the crazy simplicity of it. The snowshoe seems to open the way to a whole new world of safe and sanitized exploration. (I do not mention the possibility that a blizzard may obliterate your tracks, thereby prolonging your pickle. Sometimes it is best not to overwhelm young minds with too much information at a time.)

An hour out we stop for a snack. The kids are covered with snow. We chat about great issues, issues like the conjectured hibernation of woodchucks, and the advisability of eating icicles. Raisins and lemon drops make the rounds. High above us behind a thinly forested ridge, a granite sky beckons through lightly falling snow. To some the ridge looks impossibly distant. I sweeten the pot by putting up the irresistible reward of a Catskill summit. At the very top, I announce, there will be a tree. Attached to the tree there will be an orange box. It won't be easy to locate, *amigos*, we'll have to search like starving field mice to find it. But the search will be worth our pains, because inside the box there will be a notebook, and inside the notebook you will sign your names, to prove that you are worthy.

It works. The incentive carries us upward, even as the second hour grows long and the third brings its customary measure of discouragement and doubt. Grumbles abound, complaints that my pace is mad, that the whole idea was lunacy from the start. A good sign: the sky is brightening in anticipation of our arrival. Slapping branches from our eyes, we push through a line of chubby Christmas trees. Suddenly the angle eases and we break out onto the ridge.

The sensation of floating is startling; it's the feeling you get when you step onto an escalator that isn't moving. The pain, even the memory of the pain, evaporates into thin air. Everyone is smiling, gabbing again. I brace myself stiff-armed against my knees to catch my breath. In the *Symposium* we learn that Socrates the soldier was a man of great physical as well as intellectual powers. His endurance and fortitude, Alci-

biades tells us, were unparalleled. On winter marches, when his comrades donned heavy coats and footwear of felt and fleece, the great one
chose summer togs and bare feet. Then he outmarched the others
across the ice. Shall we believe the kisser: he was the only one who enjoyed the hike?

Midday finds us alternately skimming over voluptuous cushions of
snow and plunging thigh-deep into soft powder overlying deadfalls and
dwarf firs. At their summits Catskill peaks are forested plateaus. Finding the top isn't the piece of cake it is on Everest. Here you have to
search out the one tree among hundreds whose base some sadistic
geographer has decreed to be six inches higher than the rest. Hungry
and dejected, we crash about through the snow, our quest for truth fast
running out of gas. *There is a box!* I keep shouting. *Attached to a tree!*
I can hear the derangement in my voice, and the doubt. I am no help,
of course; I have never been here before.

Find the box!

STUDENT: And what if we do not find the box, Socrates? Will life not go
    on as before? Will the earth not continue to spin happily on its axis?
SOCRATES: Surely both will go on, as you say.
STUDENT: Whether or not we persevere, then, is clearly not relevant to
    the future of life or the happy spinning of the earth. In that case per-
    haps we might just as well sit down in the snow and eat lunch.
SOCRATES: Very good. If the future of life and the spinning of the earth
    are our sole concerns, then I agree that we are foolish to continue the
    search. But tell me, might there not be a higher authority than
    either of these? What of the authority of the heart? What of the au-
    thority of the mind? Are these not the highest authorities? And if so,
    will it truly be well for us to disregard them when we are so near to
    the attainment of our goal?
STUDENT: The wind is blowing pretty hard, Socrates. My fingers are
    beginning to feel like frozen carrots.
SOCRATES: Let us consider the natures of the heart and the mind. I am

anxious to hear your position on this matter, dear friend. Do you believe you can persuade me that in our rush to accede to the authority of another, we can safely disregard the authority of these two?

STUDENT: That's quite an order, Socrates. Actually, I think I shall have a better chance of success if I take a blow here and scarf down a nice cheese sandwich.

Suddenly a shout. The box has been found! From all directions we converge on the titled fir and crowd around jabbering feverishly, as though a deserter were about to be shot. Someone pops open the door and in short order we are duly registered conquerors.

The mood shifts with the afternoon wind. In twos and threes we range over the mountaintop, savoring its delights. Our summit is every summit: it is peace and quiet, length and breadth, pure and timeless reach. It has the power to transform. My seat for lunch is a grumpy log, of Shaker design. My companions at table are Parker and Benchley, late of the Algonquin. Reports from the hinterlands filter in. Moss! Pine cones! Mice! (On one of our summits someone found a man and a woman zippered into a sleeping bag together, plainly alive.) Dave and I poke at our pipes; the sun peeps festively through the overcast. Suddenly the air hums with talk of spring and shining mountains to climb. Together the entire party walks to a small clearing and gazes out at the world below. In that moment, I believe in the deepest reaches of my heart, a breathlessness was born, a serenity they will always know.

The wind freshens and the clouds reclaim the sun. Moments later we head for home. At the head of a steep embankment, Frank McGowan, moonstruck, throws himself onto his seat. To my horror and admiration, he is suddenly rocketing down the mountainside. Backwards, sideways, left and right through the trees—

It is not something that I would have thought to do, but in a moment I am rocketing in his wake. We all are. It is exhausting, thrilling—a handy device for peeling years from your life to reveal the sleeping trickster within. Now we are all over the mountain in a search for virgin slopes. When we find one we take it in every attitude known to human-kind: feet first, head first, on our bellies kamikaze-style. Another of those strange Catskill beasts, the summit-drunk snow otter.

By late afternoon, when we reach the cars, we are soaked to the bone. Though the horsing around lacks muscle it has an exhilaration I can remember still, what a Rubinstein must feel when the concerto is safely behind him and the last quiet strains are fading in the violins. Dave and I count noses, exchange a few words, fire the engines. And then it is over and we are out the door . . . down narrow lanes in tan-dem, through dusky villages of flickering lights and hometown Satur-day night. As the sun touches the silver-blue horizon my sinuous de-scending path levels out and dissolves dismally into an on-ramp. With a sigh and a hard right I swing us south toward the city.

IV

In 1975 I retired from teaching and emigrated to California, a state whose reputation for compassion toward the poor made it an expedient destination for a man with his mind made up to become a writer. A few weeks after arriving, I returned briefly to the home country to spend Christmas with my parents in Pennsylvania. They lived on a rural road not far from Lake Erie, in the famous snow belt that in most years slam-danced in blizzards November through March. Cruel, beautiful country, and tailor-made for the holidays.

My late career was rarely in my thoughts those days, so powerful was the spell of the future. But on Christmas morning I received an unex-pected gift that jolted me happily into the past, a gift that seemed to sug-gest that my teaching legacy, if I had one, lay not at the corner of 77th and Broadway in Manhattan, but in the misty mountains that shaped the horizon behind the celebrated resorts of southeastern New York. A light snow was falling outside and the family was seated about the Christmas tree opening gifts when I heard a crunching of tires and looked out to see a Western Union van pulling into the driveway. The driver hopped out and high-stepped through the snow onto the front porch. A moment later he handed me a telegram through the front door.

CONQUERED MARCY ON THE 21ST WITH ICEAXES
CRAMPONS AND SNOWSHOES THREE FEET POWDER
MERRY CHRISTMAS
JAMIE AND HANK

Jamie Martin and Hank Tracy, two of my students at Collegiate, two stalwarts who had joined me often on the Saturday hikes in the Catskills. The Marcy mentioned in the telegram was Mount Marcy, New York's highest mountain, a fine peak in the central Adirondacks. In summer it can be ascended in a few hours on a well-graded path that wanders amiably all the way to the top. In winter the trail disappears beneath several feet of snow and the climb can test the mettle of the brassiest mountaineer. Two years earlier Dave Hertz and I, with our friend Jim Brodie, a member of the English department at Collegiate, had set out to humble the mountain in March. That was the plan. But a few minutes from the top it was we who were humbled, by a gleaming staircase of ice and hurricane winds that threatened to blast us off the peak. On our return to school we were roundly hooted for our failure.

The telegram, part gentle jibe, part bursting pride (Jamie Martin and Hank Tracy were only seventeen at the time), conveyed what I took to be exceptional news that Christmas morning. But in recent months I've solicited the recollections of many who joined me on those Saturdays in the Catskills, and learned, not entirely to my surprise, that the news from Mount Marcy had been anything but exceptional. Hank Tracy went on to become a first-class mountaineer, making scores of ambitious ascents on the great walls of Alaska, Yosemite, and the rest of the country's climbing meccas. Mike Mayers did the same, climbing hard rock and ice with some of America's finest mountaineers. Lloyd Westerman hiked Scotland coast to coast and has backpacked in the Adirondacks every summer since his sophomore year at

Collegiate; he proposed to his future wife on the summit of Giant Mountain. Kevin Miller took up dog-sled racing and sent one of his dogs to the North Pole with explorer Will Steger. Bruce Benjamin became a law enforcement officer and today heads search-and-rescue operations for the sheriff's department in the majestic mountains surrounding Aspen, Colorado. Nearly everyone I spoke with told me that he continues to visit the mountains today, some backpacking, others climbing, skiing, fishing, canoeing, or day-hiking with their families. When I asked what drew them to the mountains in the first place, several echoed the sentiments of Bruce Benjamin, who as a youngster appreciated the advantages of growing up in New York City, yet began seeking escape at every opportunity.

"The mountains meant everything to me," he told me. "They symbolized freedom, honesty, and integrity. They were somehow a constant." In retrograde motion, his discovery mirrored that of Thoreau, whose rambles in the wilds of northern Maine left him with an unexpected appreciation for the comforts of his gentle Concord. What we might call the Fundamental Theorem of Thoreau suggests that we can neither escape permanently into the wilderness nor find complete happiness in unalloyed civilization. The truth, familiar to algebra students everywhere, is that we require an exact balancing of the two sides of the equation.

"Mostly I remember walking through the beautiful Catskill Mountains with their fall colors," Hank Tracy wrote in a letter to me. "A sense of timelessness, of being part of Nature and very far from that city where we all spent too much time. At college I'd often go out for a walk in the woods or along a rural road and work out physics problems in my head. In fact I figured out the idea for my original proposition for orals at MIT walking one night. That process of walking and thinking and planning is something that I feel I developed and maybe even perfected during the descent on some of those Catskill hikes."

Carl Kissin today is a performer with an improvisational comedy troupe in New York City. In 1974 and 1975 he began to prepare for this adventurous career by recycling beloved Cheech and Chong routines (a few of us thought a trifle too many times) between breaths on trails to Catskill summits. In a tape recounting his memories of those open-air performances he recalled one unforgettable moment of silence, in "an open field filled with pristine white snow."

"We lay back in the snow, not to make snow angels but just to feel the tranquillity of the surroundings. I remember being totally knocked out by that feeling. I wasn't cold. I wanted to stay there: looking into the sky, seeing the trees around me. It was phenomenal—being taken by the spirituality and the uniqueness of the moment."

I asked the others what they thought they had learned on our outings. Some mentioned resourcefulness, others discipline, others stoicism and perseverance. Stewart Gross wrote to me of the equalizing of the trail, the disappearance of elitism and cliquishness once the city had been left behind. Ken Williams believes that friendships, self-esteem, and a will to succeed came out of his experiences, as did his awareness of and concern for the environment. In college he majored in environmental studies; after graduation his search for "a theological understanding of Creation and the Creator" led him to seminary. Today he is an ordained minister in the United Methodist Church. For a time he served a cooperative parish of seven churches in Fleischmanns, New York, in the heart of the Catskills.

None of these unlikely mountaineers born to the horizontal streets of New York City evolved a love for the mountains because he happened to go hiking as a teenager. Each had mountains in him to begin with, as he had mathematics and history and philosophy and all kinds of genius in him, as every kid does—as we all do. For Socrates was right, I think: a teacher is only a poor midwife who brings thoughts to life—who takes whatever wondrous stardust is waiting to be born and gives it a spin and sends it swirling out into the world. Recalling those long-ago Saturdays in the woods, how often I have thought of Saint-Exupéry's heartbreaking words: "Nobody grasped you by the shoulder while there was still time. Now the clay of which you were shaped has dried and hardened, and naught in you will ever awaken the sleeping musician, the poet, the astronomer that possibly inhabited you in the beginning."

And how clearly I have remembered the bleak moment at the end of the day when we drove out of the mountains and met the interstate, and two lanes became six, and a rare hush came over the car. As the road straightened before me, a deep yearning took hold—never to return to the city, to spend my life in the woods. It was a secret for me alone, a desperate plan to brighten my solitude at the wheel. The engine purred, the white line pierced the night, and one by one my passengers drifted off to sleep. As I navigated the darkness, my own eyelids heavy, I could no longer distinguish where teacher ended and mountain climber began. So tell me, dear Phaedrus, when I take you to the high-·est point of a delightful upland, there to show you what I have seen and what I love, will I be teacher or will I be mountain climber? And again, when for the same reason I conduct you along a meandering path toward reason and wisdom and light, which will I be? Your difficulty in deciding, I think, arises in the similarity of the views. For each has beauty, each has value, each seems to alter its form even as we look, as though an obscuring mist had been thrown up to conceal the true nature of the prospect from our eyes. Most marvelous of all, when we attend together and consider thoughtfully what we have seen, each has the power to guide us safely through the night.

But really, my friend, I am most anxious to hear your views on this matter. Tell me, do you think that it might be otherwise?

Pilgrimage

to

Tsoodził

*This I may say is the first time I have been at
church in California.*
JOHN MUIR, *first ascent of Cathedral Peak*, 1868

I

Bennie Silversmith: "My hair is long, to represent rain.
When you see rain beyond the horizon it looks like hair hanging down
from the sky. Sometimes when I wash my hair it gets very wild, and
then it looks like a great storm."

Turning his head, Silversmith indicates the knot at the back, a fat
barrel of jet-black hair wrapped in a thick white cord. This slightly ex-
aggerated gesture—the slow twist of the neck, the modestly bowed
head framed by an open palm—has an operatic quality about it. I take
it as a warning to stay alert, to watch for symbol and portent. Silversmith seems to be saying, "If you believe that hair is hair, my friend,
you are in for a big surprise."

"My hair knot represents the medicine bundle that our forefathers used in the healing ceremonies. Inside the medicine bundle was dirt from each of the sacred mountains. The cord I use to tie the knot is a lightning bolt, or a rainbow, or sunshine."

Bennie Silversmith is a Navajo medicine man, a towering, broad-shouldered figure in early middle age who, despite his relative youth, is known among his people for power and wisdom. Seated opposite me in his office in Window Rock, Arizona, he is a commanding presence; this is due partly to his sheer physical size, partly to the gravity with which he addresses any subject. He is outfitted in a dusty-rose down vest, blue flannel shirt, and modish tinted glasses that seem slightly out of place on the head that can so convincingly entertain a medicine bundle.

I have come to Window Rock, capital of the Navajo nation, to talk about mountains with this embodiment of lightning bolt and rainbow and sunshine. On this serene April afternoon it is sunshine that lies gently on the red-rock countryside—an exploratory, gray-tinged light still stiff from the hard days of winter. Not far from us stands the great Window Rock, an immense wall of sandstone bored through by a hole large enough to admit a small asteroid. It is a stomach-turning exercise to stand beneath the red wall, as I did earlier in the day, and to peer up into the blue kaleidoscope and contemplate the awful size of the thing; but little more so than to consider even the least celebrated vista (dry gulches strewn with down-and-out monoliths, entire longitudes of red-on-red-on-red) in this many-wondered land of the Navajo, an endless playground for the eye. For the casual spectator it is dangerous country, dangerous to the heart and to the lungs; aerobically unfit sightseers have been known to perish on the spot. In spring, when the light is tentative and the wind irritable, the land gives an unmistakable sense of movement, of proceeding to its ancient summer quarters as though it were inspired. You ride the land, foot to the floor, and you feel its heartbeat beneath you. This heartbeat resonates in Bennie Silversmith and empowers him to perform his medicine, which he does with exceeding skill, as I am soon to find out.

I have come seeking the counsel of this Navajo religious leader because I wish to visit one of the sacred mountains of his people. Like most of the world's religions (Christianity and Judaism are notable exceptions), that of the Navajo regards as holy certain high places on the earth and believes them to be inhabited by God. Silversmith's people recognize six sacred mountains. Spread over a wide area of New Mexico, Arizona, and Colorado, they mark the boundaries of the tribal homeland. Each plays an important role in the Navajo creation story and in the daily lives of traditional-minded members of the tribe. So deeply rooted is the belief that these sacred peaks are the limit of the land that some Navajo refuse to travel beyond them.

In response to a question, Silversmith describes the sacred mountains to me one by one: Dook'o'oosłííd, the mountain of abalone . . . Sis Naajiní, the mountain adorned with white shell . . . Tsoodził, the mountain of blue-green turquoise . . . Dibé Nitsaa, the mountain adorned with jet . . . Dzil Ná'oodiłii, the mountain dressed in precious fabrics . . . Ch'óol'í'í, the mountain draped in sacred jewels. "The sacred mountains are our strength," he tells me, visibly savoring the Navajo word for strength before translating it for me. Several times during our conversation Silversmith repeats the word and the context: "From the sacred mountains we get our strength."

He speaks in a slow, meandering cadence, the rhythm of a wide, deep-running river. I choose the metaphor deliberately, to suggest the nature-oriented syntax that characterizes much of his speech: an old woman's white hair is like snow; her skin is like parched summer earth. Silversmith's face remains impassive as he talks, a demeanor I take at first to denote solemnity. I quickly learn that it can also mean just the opposite. After he has described his thick head of hair as rain hanging down from the sky, I point to the beloved bald spot on the top of my head, as if to lament the poverty of the comparison.

Silversmith stares at the circle of pink for a moment. Then, dead-pan, he announces in a grave voice, "Sun . . . peeping . . . through . . . clouds." At this I laugh out loud, and the least suggestion of a smile, like the curve of the crescent moon, crosses his lips.

Silversmith's frequent references to the things of the natural world and the confidence with which he invests them with religious content and purpose reveal a conviction of God's presence in nature that I envy. My prolonged contact with mountains and wilderness has shown me that what he believes is true. Yet because I was raised a Christian, be-cause I carry in me the traces of several thousand years of Judeo-Christian tradition, I cannot fully believe in what I have discovered. When I try my skin begins to prickle and old sermons rattle in my bones. My family attended church once a week and sought God in heaven. The man who took his church in the woods was a deserter and a heathen, and a lazy one to boot. (It required strength and stamina to survive church, especially our Episcopal church, with its exhausting Olympiad of ups and downs.) My mother and father were quite liberal on most religious matters, and not much attracted to fire-and-brimstone. Yet on one thing they were unwaveringly conservative and fiery: trees were for climbing; church was for God.

For most of the past twenty-five years I have taken my church in the woods, never without a nagging suspicion that what I was doing was destined to have dreadful consequences for me somewhere down the line. From time to time I have returned to the Episcopal church out of a sense of duty and confusion, and probably fear. I always sit in a back pew and slink out early so that no one will mistake me for one of the flock. Dilatorily I have dipped my toe into the freezing waters of alien religions, most organized, a few quite the opposite. Following every baptism I return to the woods, where, God help me, I find a kingdom that seems to be spiritual, a power that seems to be infinite, and a glory that seems to be God.

Like a blind man who has learned of the stars, I inhabit a limbo between darkness and light. I continue to be amazed and embarrassed when I encounter a fellow pantheist on a trail somewhere, a fallen Lutheran or defrocked Catholic praying piously to the fir trees or babbling like some moon-faced evangelical over a sunset he reports as heavenly. In unguarded moments I do it myself and I hear the cant in every word. It is one thing to change opinions, points of view, or political parties; it is quite another to exchange old traditions for new ones. My tradition, handed down from Genesis, teaches that nature is corrupt and that humans have dominion over it for use in glorifying the Creator. My discovery is that nature is sacred and that it is nonsensical to claim dominion over such a thing, for to do so is to claim dominion over God. I wish I could bear witness to this revealed truth with the conviction of a Bennie Silversmith. Regrettably, my gospel is too recently learned for me to preach it with self-assurance. Like the good news of electricity, moving pictures, and automatic teller machines, it is gospel that still leaves me blinking my eyes.

For many Christians and Jews who have begun to see the tragic consequences of the Genesis myth—dominion gone berserk—the American Indian is emerging as a figure worthy of esteem and emulation. The Indian offers to the Euroamerican "a mystical sense of the place of the human and other living things," writes historian and philosopher Thomas Berry. "This is a difficult thing for us since we long ago lost our capacity for being present to the earth and its living forms in a mutually enhancing manner." For right-thinking Christians and Jews, the earth is object: visible, tangible, dead. "Subjective communion" with our planet, Berry suggests, is something we can learn, or relearn, from the Indian.

Such communion is manifest in the words and manner of my informant as he describes Tsoodzil, the sacred mountain I wish to visit. It is a female mountain, Silversmith says in a voice that is warm and deferential. It is a water mountain: his hand undulates in imitation of a wave. It is a mountain, he says gratefully, that was put here to enable the Navajo to be fruitful in life. How different from the mountains of the Bible—320 of them in the concordance that I checked, 95 percent "a," "the," "this," "that," or "some" mountain. Not one is described as beautiful or even mildly attractive. A few are "holy," "great," or "goodly," but only because God has momentarily put in an appearance there. In a single verse Jeremiah gives us a "destroying" mountain and a "burnt" mountain, about the closest anyone comes to dignifying a peak with a personalized description, albeit a grumpy one.

The precise location of several of the sacred mountains is a subject of debate among Navajos. Not so Tsoodzil, the sacred mountain of the south, firmly fixed in northwestern New Mexico and visible from vantage points eighty miles away. One of my reasons for calling on Silversmith is to ask him how I can approach the mountain in a way that will not be offensive to his people. This is a matter of the utmost urgency, because disrespect for and violation of Indian sacred places by non-Indians, long commonplace, have become epidemic in recent years. Countless Native American religious sites have been destroyed to make way for roads, dams, housing subdivisions, and other developments. Mountain climbers, to their huge discredit, have been among the most arrogant trespassers on Indian religious rights. Because of the religious importance of several mountains highly coveted by climbers, Indians have closed those peaks to climbing. Shiprock on the Navajo reservation in New Mexico is perhaps the prime example. Nevertheless, some climbers have ignored these bans and conducted clandestine ascents of the forbidden mountains. The superiority of the climber's purpose, apparently, outweighs any niggling and tiresome objections of the Indians on whose lands these prizes are located.

Not long ago, Tsoodzil itself was slated for development as a ski resort. But Pueblo Indians, who also attach religious significance to the peak, joined the Navajo in protest and the proposal was defeated. Lumbering and mining operations continued on the mountain unabated.

"If you go you must have a purpose," Silversmith tells me with great seriousness. "Remember that going to a mountain is like going to a man's house. You wouldn't go to a man's house without a purpose. And while you were there, you wouldn't be disrespectful or take something that wasn't yours."

He outlines some specific instructions. I am to tell the mountain my purpose in coming. I am to bless myself, say prayers, sing songs, and make an offering. Finally, he gives me a warning.

"The Spirit sent a bear to protect the mountain and bolted the mountain down to Mother Earth with lightning." Thus the danger I will face: "You may go where you want on the mountain except to the very top. It is forbidden to go to the top. The top of the mountain is guarded by the bear and the lightning bolt." It is no doubt symptomatic of my unshakable view of myself as an intruder that in the days leading up to my visit to Tsoodzil these two, the bear and the lightning bolt, will come to dominate my thoughts.

As I prepare to leave, Silversmith mentions some similarities between Navajo and Christian traditions. Each has twelve Holy People. Each has a great flood. Each has a First Man, and a First Woman who commits a major indiscretion (Navajo First Woman sleeps with Turquoise Boy, an act which, like Eve's pilfering of the fruit, has lasting and unpleasant consequences). In Silversmith's view, the similarities are not coincidental.

"Everybody talks about God in his own way. Each of us has a different name for God." Suddenly he slips into parable. "It's like a man with many children. Each child has a different way of saying 'father.' One child says Dad, another says Poppa. But no matter how many different names the children have for him there is only one father. And the father loves all of his children the same."

Outside under a dome of blue borne by six sacred mountains, I return to Window Rock for another look into its extravagant skylight. The earth pauses for breath, then catches a breeze and resumes its roll toward summer. Nearby a Navajo child plays in the shade of a ponderosa, watched over by his mother in traditional costume. The boy is beautiful but it is well not to stare; many Navajo believe there is peril in the eyes of a stranger.

But no such proscription holds for the boy. He looks at me and laughs, evidently at my beard. "Look, Mama," he cries out. "It's like grass!"

II

A few weeks earlier I had had an intuition that I should visit Tsoodził. I had been trying to write a story about Native Americans and had lost my way. Not knowing where to turn next, I had laid the story aside with a vague intention of taking it up again at a later time.

But it wouldn't leave me alone. One afternoon I took a nap, and as I was coming out of it, plying those pleasantly lapping waters that guard the boundary between sleep and wakefulness, I heard myself asking a silent question: What shall I do? And something—not a voice but a fully formed realization—came to me: Go to Tsoodził. I had had such apprehensions before and had learned to trust them. Like an unexpected letter from an old friend, they arrived with an air of mystery and excitement and faint foreboding, and they always delivered. This one was to be no exception; indeed, it heralded one of the strangest and most unforgettable experiences of my life.

Now on an April morning of black clouds and gusty winds I drove over the northern New Mexico highlands toward the mountain. It seemed a properly somber setting for attending a sacred mountain, if Tsoodził really was sacred; perhaps I had been too much conditioned by the Hollywood religious epics of my youth—*The Robe, The Ten Commandments*, and the rest—in which God always seemed to postpone his appearance until the countryside had been duly softened by a holy gullywasher. Till now the deluge had held off but the sky appeared ready to open at any moment. I made up my mind that in the event of a downpour I would drive to a suitable viewpoint for at least a gander at the mountain in liturgical garb before I returned home. As I wound my way among mesas growing darker and more menacing by the minute, I took that to be the likely order for the day.

Thirty miles from the peak I rounded a corner and felt a surge of excitement at the sudden appearance of Tsoodzil on the skyline before me. An ancient volcano just over eleven thousand feet in height, Tsoodzil has managed through the eons to maintain the classical lines of its youth: smooth, symmetric, gradually rising through deep forests to a conical snow-covered summit. Unlike mountains formed by uplift and folding, Tsoodzil stands alone, unobstructed by intervening foothills. Studying it now, I thought how natural it is that mountains should be regarded as sacred. In the cluttered world of topographical ups and downs they stand head and shoulders above the rest. The eye is drawn to them. Borges wrote that everywhere on earth all plains are the same but no two hills are alike. Who but a Nebraskan would disagree? Reaching the top of such an eminence is an ordeal, like creeping to Lourdes on your knees. And then the summit, zealously guarded by lightning bolts and bears. Surely this is the home of the gods!

I turned north onto national forest land. The road exited the bleak altiplano and inched upward into a mixed forest of ponderosa pine and white, bare-limbed aspen. In early spring the aspen looked chilly without their manic cha-cha leaves. At intervals I came upon bombed-out slopes where loggers had snatched acres of trees at a swipe. Here was the opposing view of Tsoodzil, the unholy mountain as object, storehouse of riches, servant to the people. On Tsoodzil recent plunder has included pumice, coal, and uranium to fuel nuclear weapons. Imagine Chartres with broken windows, Saint Peter's with a mineshaft kicked through the chancel, the Wailing Wall tumbled for molybdenum. I was pleased to see that on this day, at least, the engines of sacrilege would be idle. With rain threatening, no one was clear-snatching trees today. As I drove higher on a dead-end road I grew more and more certain that my pilgrimage to Tsoodzil was to be a solitary one.

The paved road turned to dirt. A curious glow illuminated the forest ahead. I slowed and squinted through the windshield. I was startled to see a narrow column of sunlight slanting down on the mountainside ahead. As I entered the brightness the sky above me cleared to a spotless blue. The clearing appeared so quickly it reminded me of a window opening in the solid overcast. I thought: How odd and how fortunate.

The spotlight followed me up the mountain. Several miles farther along and perhaps two thousand feet below the summit, rounded islands of old snow began appearing among the trees. Higher still, one island joined the next and soon the character of the landscape had changed completely. The mixed groundcover had turned to white, whole hillsides of evergreens were leaning in the wind, and snow banners were spinning from the treetops. To my delight I saw that I had rediscovered winter.

Several inches of fresh powder lay on the road, unmarked by footprints or tire tracks. I drove on a short distance. Then, below a steep, icy grade that my spinning wheels were unable to negotiate, I pulled off the road and parked.

During the drive up the mountain I had promised myself that I would be cautious, and now was the time to begin, to consider alternatives, to measure the wind, to devise a careful plan for the hours ahead. A lone man with a small car on a snowy dead-end road in inclement weather at ten thousand feet on a wild mountain in resurrected winter—let's be sensible about this!

Being sensible never entered my mind. I was so staggered by the snow, the trees, the whole razzle-dazzle, that I practically flew through the car door. Outside in shirt sleeves I stood shivering in the chill air, scanning a mountainside that looked endless in its towering trees. By now the friendly window above me seemed a natural feature of my surroundings, and I ceased to be aware that it could close as quickly as it had opened. I pulled on my down jacket and retrieved my rucksack from the trunk of the car. Judging that I would be on top of the mountain in under two hours, I tossed out everything but a snack, a bottle of water, mittens, and a hat. I checked the zippered compartment at the top of the pack to be sure that it contained the offerings I had brought for the mountain. Then I locked the car and in a choppy wind headed up the road.

The way led upward along a shelf between a steep hillside and a deep ravine carved by a mountain brook. The hillside looked intriguing, so, impulsively, I abandoned the road and took to the sloping forest, a dimly lit cathedral of Engelmann spruce heady with the fragrance of evergreen.

The new angle punched me at once in the chest. I stopped to catch my breath. Then at a slower pace I resumed the climb. I heard the crunch of my boots kicking rhythmically into the snow, and I heard the sound of my voice singing:

> Mountain of beauty,
> Mountain of trees,
> Mountain of snowfall,
> Mountain of rocks . . .

I felt foolish at first, and fraudulent. Singing to a mountain isn't my way, and what is more dishonest than a dishonest pilgrim? But Bennie Silversmith had directed me to sing and so I sang, in the same cooperative spirit that had once led me to don a yarmulke, equally self-consciously, at the wedding of a Jewish friend. In both instances, as a designated if not very faithful Episcopalian, I felt embarrassed but at the same time liberated, suspending judgment and trusting in the genius of another.

> Mountain of blue sky,
> Mountain of swallows.

I sang about what I saw, seeking out new sights to inspire the lyrics of my song. In doing so I tuned in to the shadowy underworld of the mountain I might have missed had not the hard rules of lyric writing demanded that I stay alert.

> Mountain of gray moss,
> Mountain of mouse tracks.

Great music, I suspect, is written at sea level. The higher I climbed and the more breathless I became, the less tuneful was my song. Somewhere in the midst of this rapidly deteriorating musical comedy I realized that I had forsaken melody altogether. I was no longer singing, I was chanting.

In a small clearing among the trees I paused for rest. As I sipped from my water bottle I felt the Navajo's remaining instructions nagging at me. I procrastinated. At last, buckling under, I spoke a short prayer, aiming in the manner of a grievously nearsighted archer to bless myself and my journey. Frighteningly exposed, unprotected by worshippers in surrounding pews, I groped for words. As I explained my purpose in coming here, perhaps to God's very bosom, I heard the bare, pathetic emptiness of my prayer. "Make me worthy of—what . . . I came—I've come here because I feel, well, drawn somehow . . . I'm trying to write this—thing, and I thought, maybe—anyway, help me . . ."

The words hurt. I cringed, fretted that someone might have heard me speak.

The window in the sky slammed shut. The light that had lit the way winked out. A pointed wind, newly bitter, stole into the clearing. I looked up the slope and saw an overturned trainload of fog spilling down the mountain; as if seeking me out, it parted and enveloped me. The suddenly disaffected trees receded into nebulous gray.

I didn't think of turning back. On the contrary, my desire to continue only sharpened. As I climbed higher the fog grew thicker, the snow deeper and softer. I began sinking in to my calves, then my knees. I knew I could not continue for long, for I was fast becoming exhausted. I plunged in, fought for breath, stepped up, plunged in, fought for breath. As I was approaching the limit of my endurance, Bennie

Silversmith's words suddenly came to me, reminding me silently of the mountain's ultimate gift. Scarcely realizing what I was doing, I began to chant anew:

> Mountain of beauty,
> I need your strength.

It was a plea for something I could not supply myself and without which I could not go on. Dimly I imagined that my only hope lay in a revitalized set of leg muscles, little realizing that the true source of strength was the mountain itself.

I kicked into the snow. My boot penetrated an inch or two and stopped. I blinked. I stepped up and felt a solid layer of snow grab hold beneath me. I took another step. The result was the same: instead of plunging in to the knee I again hit bottom at once. Feeling relief immediately, I stood up on a solid, secure snow cover of perfect consistency—hard enough to support me, just soft enough to crack at the surface to provide purchase and, equally important, to form discernible footprints which, when the time came, I could follow through the fog back to my car.

I was too tired to be amazed, but I did register a clear understanding that I was not alone on this venture. I remained confident of my safety but not unapprehensive. And as I climbed higher, further extended with each step, I occasionally glanced back to be certain that the indispensable footprints, my lifeline to safety, were visible behind me.

> Mountain of firm snow,
> Mountain of clear tracks . . .

In his discussion of mysticism in *The Varieties of Religious Experience*, William James concludes that mystical states add a "supersensuous" meaning to the ordinary outward data of consciousness. "Facts already objectively before us fall into a new expressiveness and make a new connection with our active life." Through most of the day I was aware that I had crossed an invisible line between the intelligible and the transcendent, and that what had begun as an ordinary hike up a mountain had become a spiritual experience. Extraordinary coincidence could explain most of what happened, but not my clear perception that coincidence explained none of it. In James's notion of the supersensuous quality of mystical states I find a perfect explanation for the change that came over me as I climbed higher and higher into the fog toward the summit of Tsoodził. My awareness of physical discomfort vanished. I climbed effortlessly, with no need for rest. Entering a state of acute sensual awareness, I heard in the ethereal silence an allusiveness—something conversing with me—and saw what was going on behind the fog, and I tasted and smelled the air and understood it as an extension of myself rather than something separate. Coincidence or accident or light-headedness might be proposed to explain some of this. Yet how shabby and inadequate these rationalizations seem when measured against the Navajo explanation for what I experienced: Tsoodził is sacred.

At some point I moved out of the forest onto an open, treeless slope. Here fog and snow blended, creating a dizzying continuum of white. Nowhere did shadows render clues to distances or depths. Up, down, left, right were all the same. Ahead I could see perhaps fifteen feet, behind, dimly, my two or three most recent footprints. The world was shapeless. I seemed to be afloat.

My only fear, a curious but under the circumstances quite well-founded one, was that I might stumble accidentally onto the top of the mountain. In my reverie I had not forgotten the medicine man's warning against climbing to the summit of Tsoodził. So limited now was the visibility that it seemed possible that I could take a step on the gradually declining slope and find I had no more steps to take. I began moving one step at a time—up a foot, stop, stare into the fog to be certain there was more mountain up there somewhere, then up another foot.

The tension was exhilarating. The mountaineer in me badly wanted the summit, yet I firmly believed that were I to reach the top I would suffer some terrible calamity. The trick, as always, was to come as close as possible to the line without stepping over it.

For some minutes I inched myself higher, savoring every moment. Finally I came to a spot where a short, steep slope rose up beside me into the fog. It topped out beyond sight at what I knew intuitively was the highest point of the mountain. It was there that I stopped, certain I had gone as high as I dared. And it was there, as I paused for my first breath in many minutes, that I clearly and unmistakably heard the roar of the bear standing on the summit of Tsoodzil.

The sound came out of the fog, perhaps thirty feet above me. It was loud and full-throated, and it terrified me. I had no doubt about the source of the sound. Standing there weak-kneed and probably too white-faced to have been distinguished from my surroundings, I sputtered to myself, "Jesus Christ, there's a bear up there!"

A moment of silence, then, a few yards to my left, a hail of rocks came crashing down the mountain. Despite my distress I felt certain that the rocks posed no danger to me. I watched as one by one they bounded harmlessly past me and disappeared into the fog below.

I held my breath, half expecting to hear a deep voice calling out my name. But the mountaintop again grew silent, and the momentary fear I had felt passed as quickly as the volley of rocks.

I knelt in the snow. From my pack I removed the offerings I had brought for the mountain—a small silver coin and a sliver of wood, a homecoming of sorts, a step toward putting the mountain together again. I said a word of thanks for the privilege of coming to this place and prayed for a safe descent to my car. Then, purely on impulse, I asked for a sign.

Like climbing past an overhanging roof, a dangerous and utterly committing act. Asking for a sign sets one on an irreversible course, laying open the possibility of shattering, irreconcilable failure. Should the sign fail to appear, the object of one's supplication is revealed as a false god. There is no denying it, no explaining it away as a mistake or a failure in communication. Only once before had I done such a thing, and I had immediately been rewarded. Now, near the bare summit of a mountain dangerously deficient in potential sign material, I did it again. Done in the right spirit, I think, this is not a calling of God's bluff but, rather, an act of prodigious faith. Of course, one says with supreme confidence and surely not wishing to be disappointed: God will deliver. I said my piece, then stood and began preparing calmly for my descent.

A moment later it began to snow. From out of the fog above me came an onslaught of great white marvelous flakes, feather-light, blizzard-thick. There were no warning shots, no genteel messenger flakes announcing what was to come. It wasn't pouring snow and then it was. I accepted this sudden storm quite happily. When I realized it was self-induced, I laughed.

And then, of course, realized my dilemma. I glanced down at the first of the footprints leading off the mountain. Already it was partially filled with snow. In a sudden panic I threw my pack over my shoulder and jumped off down the slope. I descended sideways, scanning the terrain beyond my lower foot for the reassuring shadow of the footprint below. The imbroglio of white, the already confusing fog and ground cover now complicated by a downfall of snow: my head spun. Each footprint seemed harder to spot than the one before. I started moving faster and more carelessly, watching helplessly as the sharply etched prints of my ascent began rounding and filling, sinking inexorably into the snow cover.

My glasses fogged up. Cursing, I stopped. With a corner of my handkerchief I attempted to remedy the problem, succeeding brilliantly in compounding it instead. Now I looked out on an immaculately white world coated with an obscuring film of moisture.

My heart sank. The zeal and the certainty that had brought me this far had vanished. I knew I would never outrun the snow. Even had I been able to, I knew from experience that racing pell-mell down a mountain is a sure prescription for disaster. Standing on that bare slope carpeted in featureless white, robbed of the footprints I had counted on to show the way home, I began to wonder if I might not be in something of a jam.

I swore again and registered a long moment of foreboding. Dutifully but without much conviction, I began hammering out a plan. And then suddenly, as abruptly as the snow had begun to fall, I felt myself growing calm and confident again. Not because of the plan, which had gone nowhere. But as the snow poured down and the route dropped off below me as bewilderingly as ever, I realized that the solution to my problem lay not in seizing control of the mountain, my instinctive reaction on most occasions of high drama, but in allowing the mountain to seize control of me; to put it another way, that it was necessary for me only to trust. This method of saving one's skin is not covered in most mountaineering manuals, nor is it the one I would normally recommend. But normality had disappeared long before, and trusting somehow seemed right.

My fear passed at once. Gazing about, I grasped what an extraordinary moment it was. Then, slowly and calmly, I began moving down the slope. I had no clear idea of where I was going but I understood what I needed to do. A few steps into my descent I began to sing:

> Mountain of beauty,
> I need your strength.

Once only. As the final word departed my lips the snow stopped. The fog lifted. The window above me flew open, revealing its circle of impeccable blue.

I found nothing peculiar in any of this. Quite the contrary, what happened seemed as natural as the perfect spring day I enjoyed during the pleasant stroll back to my car.

Only one of Bennie Silversmith's prophecies, if that is what they were, remained to be fulfilled. Some friends to whom I have told this story insist that because what happened next did not happen on the summit of Tsoodzil, where it was foretold, I reveal a zealot's blindness by including it in the story. They say that I am fitting the evidence to the theory rather than the other way around.

They are right. Because I believe that the experience I have described was in some way a religious one intended to reveal the sacredness of Tsoodził, I have—not bent the evidence to fit the theory, but allowed metaphor to creep into my tale. When the Navajo said *summit*, I maintain, he had in mind a wider meaning than the one we customarily understand. This was perfectly consistent with his practice throughout our conversation. By *summit* he meant not simply the topmost point of the peak but a wider area, perhaps the entire mountain.

Certainly that part of it where the dirt road joined the pavement and where later that day in a light rain under dark skies I drove somewhat dazedly down the mountain. The high desert lay before me and beyond that the valley of the Rio Grande and home. I had been thinking about my waking dream of a few weeks before and now, on the summit of the mountain, I spoke aloud: Grant me the strength to write my story well. And from out of the darkness there came a light. It was brilliant, silver-white, and arrow-straight, and it was a bolt of lightning that nearly tore the roof off the car. Simultaneously a deafening clap of thunder resounded in my ear. The following morning I took up my story with renewed purpose and finished it not long after, perhaps gaining the strength to do so from the single bolt of lightning I observed during my visit to Tsoodził.

III

It was paradise where they were born. There creation was good, the trees were pleasant to the sight, the water was pure and it nourished the garden that was their home. The name of the garden was Eden, a word that meant "delight" . . . the Garden of Delight. And God gave them dominion over the fish of the sea and the fowl of the air and over every living thing that was in the garden. But they did not realize their good fortune and they did not understand the nature of consequences, and they sinned. And because of their sin they were sent out of the garden into a cursed wilderness choked with thistles and thorns. And he was condemned to a hard life and an early grave, and she to bearing her young in sorrow. And paradise was lost and man and woman debased and nature corrupted. So it was and so His followers, Christians and Jews, believed.

A powerful and haunting story, one that usefully explains much about our world and its inhabitants. And one that, like all creation myths, is full of holes. If Eden was created perfect, how then did it contain evil? Ah, well, you see . . . For the truly pedantic there is the problem of the rib: If God snatched a rib from Adam to make Eve, why are men and women accoutered equally in ribs?

And the major hole: If God's creation was so good, why did He put it in the hands of certifiably sinful humans, thereby sowing it with the seeds of its own destruction? Why did He put these demonstrably irresponsible creatures in charge of the Cedars of Lebanon, the Rhine River, Glen Canyon, the green hills of Kentucky, passenger pigeons, elephants, Love Canal, the air over Los Angeles, the late, lamented fish of the lakes of the Adirondacks—these glories of His creation—to do with as they willed?

It is hard to believe that God intended any of this. And as the destructive consequences of the Genesis myth have become increasingly apparent during these declining years of the twentieth century, a few theologians have begun a crash search for a new reading of the sacred texts, one that might preserve the faith without destroying the earth. Matthew Fox, the Dominican scholar, has achieved a considerable following among liberal Christians for his reinterpretation of much of Judeo-Christian tradition. While acknowledging that the nature-is-corrupt doctrine has dominated thought and action through the centuries, Fox insists that the true spirit of Western religion is ecological. It is a spirit that respects God's creation, recognizes our deep connections with it, and takes joy from this gift which is indeed sacred. Fox numbers among the proponents of this view Abraham, David, Jesus,

Saint Benedict, Saint Thomas Aquinas, and a host of other big names, all of whom have somehow been drowned out by the Huns and Vandals of the faith.

Like most religious debates, this one promises to be endless. For a floundering Christian like myself, one casting about for a permutation of Christianity that is responsible to the exigencies of the modern world without being faithless to the traditions of the ancient, there is much to be gained, I think, in abandoning all hope that a fresh look at Genesis will magically turn up a previously unrecognized *Walden*. Instead, ask why that text's undeniably anti-nature bias came to be incorporated into it in the first place. When contrasted with the inspiration for the nature-celebrating creation myths of the American Indian, such an approach, I believe, can lead Christians and Jews to a deeper and more respectful understanding of the beliefs and religious practices of that vast majority of Native American tribes that honor nature, and at the same time cast a new light on vexatious Genesis, one that will allow its veneration without being blind to its shortcomings.

At the farthest reaches of their cultural memories, thorns and thistles haunted the writers of the opening pages of the Bible. And for good reason: thorns and thistles defined the land of their ancestors, the land where their traditions were born. In time it would be called the Fertile Crescent, the birthplace of Western civilization. A narrow semicircular plain, it began in the country we know today as Iraq and followed the courses of the Tigris and Euphrates rivers north and west into Syria, before curving south through Lebanon, Jordan, and Israel. But before 15,000 B.C., during those eons of scorching sun and hot winds when the observing mind inferred from its surroundings the truths it would package as myth, the crescent was an unkind land. It supported few plants and animals, and never in dependable supply. Drought was a never-ending curse. Here began the horror of wilderness that we read in the Bible, and the notion of water as God's greatest gift. To the hunter/gatherers who scratched out a living from this desolation, these prototypes of the disgraced Adam and Eve, land was never bountiful;

in its natural state it was harsh and unmerciful. All of them must have felt that if the land were ever to be generous, it would have to be changed.

It was necessity, then, not God, that granted these people dominion over creation. The reclamation began with the animals. They could not have been better placed: pigs, goats, sheep, cattle, all wild, all rapidly domesticated to serve their self-appointed masters. (How essential the cooperation of chance: had they been lions and tigers the revolution might never have begun.) By 6,000 B.C.—five thousand years before Genesis—the hunter/gatherers had put down roots. By genius or by accident, some brave Prometheus among them had stolen a law of nature. Now in place of thorns and thistles stood fields of hardy, totally unnatural species of grain. Hybrids, better than the real stuff, fashioned by the hand of man.

To those who had accomplished this human miracle, the sight of the recreated landscape must have stirred not only the heart but the imagination. Soon, instead of consuming the entire harvest these enterprising architects of change, now farmers, began saving some of it, replanting it for later use. Daniel Zohart of Hebrew University has suggested intriguingly that this step may represent the first instance of humans working against nature for their own benefit.

A seed was planted. The great harvest of the millennium brought forth not only newly created grains but the earth-shattering realization that the thorns could be defeated, nature controlled, happiness and peace of mind wrenched from the wicked land. By 5,000 B.C.—four thousand years before Genesis—the farmers of the increasingly fertile crescent had discovered irrigation and turned it successfully against the infernal drought. By 4,000 B.C. they were plundering the forests of the Zagros Mountains for wood to burn in their smelting furnaces. By 3,500 B.C. the first battle of the wilderness was over. The once wretched plain was now green and generous, and the land was called Babylonia. There farmers tended wide fields of domesticated grains fed by reservoirs and irrigation canals. From herds of docile stock quartered just beyond their doorsteps they collected milk, meat, wool, and other valuable products. Some they used themselves; the rest they sold in the marketplaces of Uruk, Ur, and Nippur, vital cities of 20,000 inhabitants that had arisen out of the cruel soil of the crescent. The grand march of Western civilization had begun. Thanks be to God!

Hardly. All of this was possible, the land had become productive, *because humans had made it so*. God admitted as much. In the Babylonian creation story, Marduk, the chief god, cultivates a plot of ground. To water it he constructs an irrigation canal. To drain it he digs a trench. In their wisdom the Babylonians granted Marduk dominion over the land.

The Hebrews trace their ancestry back to this metasphere, to the city of Ur, to a people who seized control over creation. During his long wanderings Abraham traversed the entire crescent, beginning in Ur, migrating up the Euphrates to Syria and then down to Canaan. The events of the first eleven chapters of Genesis, first recorded between 900 and 600 B.C., correspond in time to the half-millennium that began to unfold in Babylonia about 2,900 B.C., some 1,000 years after Ur and Uruk were founded. Who can be surprised that the stories that inspired the myth of the garden portrayed nature as accursed or humans as the masters of creation? Who can wonder that the God of the Hebrews was not to be found in the land? The land was abominable! To the authors of Genesis it was axiomatic that only by controlling nature could a people survive, raise families, serve God—even invent writing and parchment upon which to record their story of creation. It was thorns and thistles that led to Ur and what came after, a civilization that could understand the land in its natural state not as the home of God but as the dwelling-place of despair.

For the ancient peoples of North America the land was generous, and their creation stories reflect that fact. Wild game was abundant. In most places water was plentiful. In the forests and on the plains, edible plants grew naturally and in profusion. There was no need for these people to plant fields, herd cattle, plunder forests, or dig canals, and, indeed, they did almost none of this. Of animals they domesticated only the dog and the turkey; of plants just three, maize, squash, and one type of bean (tomatoes, peppers, and potatoes originated in Central and South America). Unlike the inhabitants of the Fertile Crescent, Native Americans never discovered the wheel, the lever, the wedge, the screw, the smelting of metal, or phonetic writing; they developed almost nothing that is regarded by Euroamerican authorities as emblematic of civilization.

And why should they have? They lived in paradise. Through some accident of truly cosmic proportions, they had not been expelled from the garden. For these dwellers of the sacred land, Eden was not a lost dream. It was home.

. . . and it was good. And God said, Let the earth bring forth aspens and oaks and cottonwoods and prickly cactus and columbines and snapdragons and mockingbirds that sing in the golden light of dawn. And let there be blue lakes and emerald valleys and verdant plains and redrock canyons and deserts the color of rainbows. And let the rivers teem with trout and the plains with bison and antelope, and let the trees hang heavy with apples and plums and pears and all manner of fruit. And let the streams run clear and the rain fall cool and the wind blow sweet with the aroma of all that is in My garden.

And let there be mountains tall and shining, and let them have pines and cedars to adorn them, and deer and eagles to make their homes upon them, and granite walls and ridges to impart them with majesty. And let the people gaze upon the mountains and be joyful and know that I am there. For I shall dwell upon the mountaintops forever.

In so blessed a land it is unimaginable that the Indians should not have found God in the rocks and in the trees and on the high peaks. Their myths confirmed God's presence in creation, ratifying the Indian's sacred relationship with the earth as Judeo-Christian myth did not. That the Indian never evolved a scrupulous concept of private land ownership, investment property, or mortgage interest payments has been cited by some authorities as further proof of the poverty of Native American culture. Understood as a natural consequence of the Indian's belief in the sacredness of the land, these omissions seem no more surprising or uncivilized than the capitalist revolution that occurred in Babylonia around 2,300 B.C., when private ownership of land was recognized for the first time. Babylonians could buy land without buying God, a business transaction that was not possible in North America.

Not, at least, until the disciples of an alien tradition arrived with their hymnals and their crinoline and their distantly wrought understanding of the economy of the world. They imposed their order on the new land, an act of grotesque sophistry, for myth is of a place: here were not thorns and thistles, here was a powerful and giving land. It was inevitable that their failure to understand this would have tragic and perhaps irreversible consequences.

It would be foolish to argue that Genesis is wrong; on the contrary, it faithfully and wisely bears witness to the traditions of its time and place. Christians and Jews who love nature need to recognize this and to respect the integrity of the story. It documents the truth of the land of their faraway beginnings.

But not the truth of America. It would be well for those of us who are new to this place to listen at last to the stories and observe the ways of the continent's indigenous peoples, whose traditions sprang from the land and who have one incontrovertible boast that Christians and Jews cannot make: they were not expelled from the garden. Surely that is an achievement that merits our respect and our awe. We Euroamericans do not need to become Indians in order to see the propriety of yielding to Native Americans their sacred places and returning those taken from them. Nor to open our eyes to the entire world of nature, not only the shining mountains and stormy oceans, which are easy to see, but the nature in our backyards, which is not. With that we may begin finding God in unaccustomed places: in the ravaged tenements of the sacred inner cities, in the foul waters of the sacred streams and rivers, in the stinking soils of the sacred hazardous waste dumps. Tsoodzil, the mountain of blue-green turquoise, is everywhere. We may be thankful to recognize this at last and to know that some of the garden remains. Now let us watch over it and tend it with care. Having lost paradise once, surely we do not want to lose it again.

Landscape
of the
Settled Heart

Rise free from care before dawn, and seek adven-
tures. Let the noon find thee by other lakes, and
the night overtake thee everywhere at home.
HENRY DAVID THOREAU, *Walden*

One of the many oddities about the sport of mountaineering
is that although it is practiced by few and is unintelligible to most non-
practitioners, it possesses an iconography that is universally known and
appreciated. Who does not understand the symbolism of the ice axe,
that canny product of human ingenuity which allows the climber to
overcome obstinate nature, or the rope, the umbilical cord through
which the life spirit of one climber passes to the other? What tradition
has not employed *ascent* as a metaphor for passage to a more godlike
plane, or to a state of perfect self-actualization where the soul is puri-
fied, the mind released, or the epic journey completed?

Most widely recognized of all must be the symbol of the mountain itself, variously seen as the unreachable, the inscrutable, the fearful, or the obstacle to be overcome. Thanks to George Leigh Mallory's famous explanation for his (to the nonclimber) baffling compulsion to climb, the mountain has entered the public consciousness, too, as a symbol of that which justifies itself. The not altogether happy result of Mallory's achievement is that it is a rare week that passes when one does not hear some cheerful proselyte singing the praises of mud wrestling or beekeeping, or endure a commercial promoting something otherwise utterly unpromotable, like psychic dentistry, *because it is there*!

A rich lexicon of symbols, yet one that is incomplete, for somehow it overlooks that emblem of mountaineering which better than any other clearly and concisely expresses the climber's mysterious attachment to the high peaks. I sometimes find, perched atop a mountain, that my gaze is drawn not only outward and upward but downward too, in search not of sweeping panoramas of snowy peaks but of the tiny, brightly colored tent where the day's long and hopeful journey began. Usually it is obscured by trees or rocks or some other intervening obstacle. But occasionally I can pick it out at the edge of the forest or in the midst of a sprawling glacier, the crown jewel in a sparkling tiara of snow. When I spot it I invariably let out a shout. Unless they are otherwise occupied, my companions usually scramble to my side and follow my pointing finger until they, too, see the tent standing far below. A bit wistfully we gaze in silence. To think—we've come all that way! The sight is always a mixed blessing, for along with its heartening glimpse of the end of the road it lays out a disquieting view of the road itself and of the hazards we must overcome before our travels are over.

For most of the years that I played this game I regarded it as nothing more than a pleasant mountaintop diversion. But on an eye-opening climb in the northern Purcell Range of British Columbia a few years ago, for the first time I saw the search as more than a game and the object of the search as more than a tent. With my friend Kai Wiedman I had flown to Calgary and rented a car for a drive over the Canadian

Rockies and down the western slope into the valley of the Columbia River. There we picked up a rough and dusty road which we bumped along for the next several hours, carefree as Mister J. Thaddeus Toad on a madcap Sunday afternoon outing. Our destination was a remote area of wondrous needlelike peaks called the Bugaboos.

Although it is one of the most spectacular mountain regions anywhere, the Bugaboos are little visited by tourists, which makes them all the more alluring to climbers. Not only is the road rough, dusty, and unimproved by shopping malls, it leads—according to most canons of opinion—nowhere. At road's end lies no alternative but to continue by foot along an arduous backpacking trail that ascends the valley of the Bugaboo Glacier, eventually via ladders on the walls, into a vertical Plutonian wilderness offering the visitor but a single conceivable means of entertainment: mountain climbing. The Bugaboos seem to have been created for mountaineers alone, a grand gift of skyscraping spires rising straight out of perpetual snow: Colorado with solitude, Yosemite Valley with ice, paradise with clean granite walls.

At the edge of the final trees we pitched our tent. And, having done so, underwent that transformation of mind that marks any extended sojourn in the mountains: as the days passed and we settled in to our ever more congenial surroundings, climbing seemed less and less like sport and more and more like what we did in life. Each morning we rose well before dawn, threw down a cold breakfast, and ventured out into the hostile, pitiless world. Each night, chastened, grouchy, and sore, but enormously pleased with ourselves, we trudged back to camp as though we'd just survived a hard day at the office. Jokes over the back fence with neighbors, too much Yukon Jack in a green plastic cup, Pasta Something for dinner, then early to bed to catch a few winks before starting in all over again. In the Bugaboos we led a rigorously circumscribed existence in an abode of unconditional acceptance. I knew my place (mountains by day, blue tent by night), and that knowledge instilled in me a feeling of utter contentment.

One morning we set out to climb the west ridge of a striking pyramid of pearly granite called Pigeon Spire. It is an easy climb by Bugaboo standards, which is not to say deficient in lovely places from which to fall. For a modestly skilled climber like myself, ever ready to oblige at such places, the ridge offered a perfect climb—challenging but well within my capabilities, airy but with plenty of handles to grab when knees began to rattle.

We climbed gamely, toasted our blunders and indiscretions as though they were virtues, hooted camp songs into the wind. The views on both sides of the narrow ridge were magnificent, the rock beneath us was firm and gnarly as a peach pit. We climbed with the sun, peeping over more and more distant ridges into inviting countries beyond. I remember the sight of my friend above or below me, grinning ear to ear, ridiculing my clumsiness in the approved fashion, urging me on, and the unparalleled pleasure of working in concert with him—the exhilarating shift from real time into the timelessness of total immersion in a task.

Several hours out, we topped the first and lowest of the spire's three summits. We took a short break, then descended a ramp to the base of a steep wall that rose toward the mountain's middle peak. From a distance the wall looked hard. After procrastinating suitably I stepped up, slipped around a corner, and to my great relief happened onto a surprise crack that led easily upward. My pleasure at finding the crack, however, was short-lived. Moments after exiting at the top I came upon a fiercely exposed skyway, the sight of which made my head swim. Horizontal, perhaps fifteen feet in length and a few inches in width, it offered little margin for error.

At sea level, as they say, an acrophobiac could handle it blindfolded. Observing the smiling glacier beckoning far below on either side of my proposed route, I eschewed the blindfold, choosing instead eyes as big as fried eggs. My final act before embarking was to shout my last will and testament down to Kai, leaving him, as I recall, all of my remaining dried apricots. Then I took a deep breath and scampered across. To my amazement I arrived on the far side in one piece.

Kai soon joined me, bringing the troubling news that halfway across the knife edge he had been able to stifle a gigantic yawn. We traversed the middle summit, then descended a groove to the base of the final tower. Here Kai took the lead. After dropping down and around to the left, he mounted a short face to a horizontal crack in the wall. Jamming his fingers into the crack, he eased his way along the base of the tower till he reached an easy gully leading upward. That was the end of the difficulties. Five minutes later we were stretched out in the sun on the tiny knob at the top of the spire.

With the uncertainties of the ascent behind us, we enjoyed our well-earned rewards: rest, satisfaction, small talk, and a gleaming panorama of peaks and glaciers few have been privileged to see. I felt happy, at peace in the company of mountains. Then, as if not quite finished with summit business, I allowed my gaze to slip downward . . . over the edge, down the sweeping wall of rock, down the crazily tumbling glacier, into the trees—

I saw it clearly, a tiny blue dot at the limit of my sight. Impulsively I let out a whoop. Suddenly, peering down from my giddy perch in the sky, I understood for the first time that here at my side was not friend but family, that what we were doing was not climbing but living; and, most of all, that the tiny blue dot waiting for us so staunchly and faithfully at the end of the day was not a tent at all, was not even shelter or refuge or safety. It was our home.

Americans are a rootless bunch. Half a millennium after Columbus, those of us whose ancestors were not native to these shores still suffer from what the Polish Nobel laureate Czeslaw Milosz, himself freshly uprooted to the United States, labels darkly "the immutable violence of new beginnings." We endure this violence in manifold ways but never more destructively than in our relationship with the earth beneath us, this newfound land whose contours, textures, and ageless truths remain alien to us even today. Restless by destiny, lighting out for the next territory and then the one beyond, we fail to achieve perfect intimacy with any quarter of the land. The imprint we leave behind us is not one of kindly use, as Wendell Berry would have it, but of uprooted trees and tire tracks. Like the irresolute suitor who grows edgy at the prospect of commitment, we move on, as yet incapable of Gary Snyder's "radical act" of living in one place for the rest of our lives. Figures compiled by the Center for the Study of Population at Florida State University tell us that the average American inhabits thirty dwellings in a lifetime; my own record so far is twenty-four apartments and houses in fourteen cities and six states. Tirelessly we plod from block to block, from city to city, searching not for a plot of land to tend and to love but for escape, better jobs, warmer climates, higher pay, lower property taxes.

But not, I think, for homes. The distinction between rootlessness and homelessness is important but one that we commonly gloss over. As a result, we anguish more over our supposed homelessness than we need to. "ROOTS," a popular magazine emblazons on its front cover: "A restless nation searches for a place to call home." Restless we are and bereft of permanent habitations, but as nomads have always known, neither bears in the slightest on the search for home. Home, after all, is a stillness of the heart, not of the feet. It is no less likely to be found on a speeding train than it is in a charming Cape Cod with a white picket fence. I have known people who moved practically annually who were comfortably at home the moment they entered their new dwellings for the first time; with few exceptions, the mountaineers that I know have this capacity. Rootless they may be, but, as most of them have discovered soon after they began climbing, home is where the tent is, a movable feast celebrated anew each time they return to the mountains.

In *The Denial of Death*, Ernest Becker argued that the compelling force in our lives is the urge to be a hero. Society is a "symbolic action system," a kind of dead-serious amusement park with Ferris wheels that spin out of control and roller coasters that scare the daylights out of us and shooting galleries that parade impossible choices before our eyes; all so that we may be surrounded with glittering opportunities to act heroically. We participate in the system in order to earn a feeling of "cosmic specialness" by carving out places for ourselves in nature.

Becker did not connect this impulse with the search for home, but I think that he might have, for his phrase "carving out a place in nature" describes better than any I know the means for settling the heart. Mountaineers do it by climbing the hills and discovering a terrain that accepts them unconditionally, one where they know they belong. Others find it at the ocean, beside prairie lakes, in city parks, or in back-yard gardens. When circumstances prevent travel or obscure the earth, a simple window box planted with chrysanthemums will serve. The place that we seek may be fixed, like a window box, but more commonly it is a broad pattern of landscape, an accident of personal geography like Mary Austin's deserts and Rachel Carson's sea: where the power of nature is manifest and the earth says, Here you are welcome.

Robert Coles, that tireless observer of humankind, tells us of the poor Appalachian woman who placed her child on the ground before her and began rocking him with her bare feet. "This is your land," she said to the boy, "and it's about time you started getting to know it." That woman had a home, and so, we can be sure, did her child. Her deep sense of her place in nature transcended possessions, cultural boundaries, and physical setting; somehow she had learned to see herself as part of the scenery, allowing her to achieve what Frederick Turner identifies as "that surest of realities: the human spirit and its dark necessity to realize itself through body and place."

Having found our places, we return to them again and again. Until recently I had imagined that we did so for the remainder of our lives, but an exchange of letters with Fritiof Fryxell dispossessed me of that quaint idea. One of America's great pioneer mountaineers, Fryxell made his mark during the twenties and thirties, the mad-inventor period in American mountaineering, the era of clothesline ropes, hobnail boots, and seat-of-the-pants improvisation, when a young and ambitious climber could wander into practically any range of mountains and there find dozens of untouched walls and virgin summits on which he (it was always a he) could make a name for himself. Fryxell made his name in Wyoming's Grand Tetons, where he compiled a brilliant record of first ascents. Several of his routes are now regarded as classics.

Having climbed often in the Tetons, including more than a dozen of Fryxell's routes, I had often wondered what it must have been like to have known the range when it was young, when each bootstep took one higher into unexplored terrain. So when I learned that Fryxell, now in his eighties, was living in Illinois, I wrote him a fan letter. I wanted to thank him for opening the way to duffers like me and I hoped to coax him into spinning a few yarns about the old days. But I had a more charitable purpose in writing, too: I was sure that Fryxell must be miserable in Illinois (highest point, Charles Mound, elevation 1,235 feet). In those grim horizontal surroundings surely he would be elated to hear from someone, anyone, with news from the high country.

A few weeks later I received a generous and self-effacing reply. Fryxell thanked me for my blandishments and allowed that he was "plain lucky" to have found himself in the Tetons "when so much needed to be done." He wrote fondly but not sentimentally about those distant times. About his consignment to Illinois he evinced no note of bitterness or regret. Through this and through a later letter I learned something I had not guessed, I who had assumed that a mountaineer could not live without mountains: Fryxell was content in level Illinois not because mountains lived on in his memory, although they did; but far more significantly, because they lived on in his reality. Having long ago found his place in nature, he could never again be apart from it. Fryxell needed no mountains beckoning at his doorstep. It was enough for him simply to know that mountains exist. Armed with that knowledge he would always be among them.

It should be obvious that if the search for home is an endeavor to integrate oneself with nature, it may or may not have something to do with family, hearth, security, or any of the other attributes we traditionally associate with home, and nothing at all to do with houses. Somehow we have got it exactly backwards. We speak of the homeless, whom we should properly call the houseless, for many of those afflicted souls are blessedly settled of heart and as content with their single, ever-changing square foot of planet as the millionaire is with his thousands. These people do not need homes, they need houses. To call them houseless, however, makes all too plain not only the problem but the solution; and, even more bothersome, the implication of us the house-ful in both. Perhaps this explains our preference for *homeless*, a for-mulation that conveniently loses problem, solution, and implication in the timeless mysteries of home.

As for others of us, in our drive to be heroes we spend our early adult years collecting down payments for houses which, if we secure them, we spend our middle years stocking with families, hearths, security sys-tems, and the rest. If that is the end of it we are likely to be surprised and embittered in our old age to discover that it is we who are homeless, that far from acquiring cosmic specialness we have achieved a crippling sameness, and that a terrifying malaise stalks us into the darkness ahead. How terrible to contemplate our failures, how baffling and en-raging to observe the contented smile on the face of the poor woman of far Appalachia so masterfully rocking her child on the warm earth be-fore her.

Perhaps it seems that I am only trying to say that Earth is our home. Certainly I am happy to claim that currently fashionable address as my own, though for the same reason that I dislike the term *homeless*, I would like to see earth advocates begin advertising their client as our house. That might bring our pious sentiments down to earth, so to speak, and suggest the kind of practical solutions our current dilemma demands: Clean up your room! Tend the garden! Fix the roof!

Nevertheless, while our planetary address may be Earth, who among us is capable of finding peace on each acre of that sprawling es-tate? The view of our house from space may be stunning, but the place in nature that we seek must be sculpted on a more intimate, more hu-man scale. During the last years of his life, Joseph Pulitzer lived on

New York City's East 73rd Street in an Italian Renaissance mansion containing sixty rooms, forty-five of which he never visited. Pulitzer might properly have been chided for his colossal wastefulness, but it is easy to sympathize with his plight: his digs, like ours, were simply too large. For all our grand ideas and preposterous schemes, most of us take our greatest pleasures from our smallest ones. "The idea that everybody wants to be president of the United States or have a million dollars is simply not the case," John Berryman once told an interviewer. "Most people want to go down to the corner and have a glass of beer." Whether Joseph Pulitzer found happiness in his mostly unexplored Italian Renaissance mansion I don't know. I hope he at least found a shady corner of his garden with an olive tree and an allure he could not explain, a place to which he was drawn as some are drawn to the mountains and some are drawn to the sea. One that spoke to him as a friend, heart to heart, filling him with longing when he was absent and serenity when he was home.

In our grand earthly mansion, we seek comfortable rooms of our own.

The journey home begins when we learn to distinguish one place from another and find that some stir our imaginations more than others. Geographer Yi-Fu Tuan has coined a term for this journey: topophilia, the proclivity to grow attached to a particular landscape. Since we know that cats have favorite chairs and horses their preferred corners of the corral, we can be sure that topophilia is a characteristic we share with other living creatures. What is surprising is just how many, and how far down the ladder of life this tendency occurs. Somehow attachment to place has proven its selective value almost from the beginning of evolutionary time.

Consider the tiny planarian worm, a resident of seashore and swamp for some six hundred million years. One of the simplest forms of life on earth, the planarian enjoys neither brain, digestive system, circulation system, nor, except on occasions so rare they must surely have acquired among members of the species the status of Christmas, sex. To gather its news of the world, to think, worry, appreciate, and plan, the planarian relies on a single pair of nerves connected by two ganglia.

That is it, about a trillionth or so of what each of us can turn to the same purpose. Given these modest gifts, the planarian must have a level of awareness scarcely higher than that of the matchbox or the spoon. Yet in ways no one can fathom the little creature can learn, remember, choose sensibly, and, most important for our purposes, exhibit topophilia. Planarians prefer to eat in places they know well— comfy places, homey places. Offered food in a strange location, they'll take twice as long to begin eating as will their cousins on familiar ground. Give them an opportunity to know a spot, to stretch out and learn the lay of the land, and they'll quickly grow attached to it, taking their meals there as apparently contentedly as you or I might in our favorite chair at the dining room table. It is pleasant to speculate that planarians may have a rudimentary understanding of home, and that home would live forever in their hearts, if only they had hearts.

For those of us who are higher on the ladder of life, the task of finding our preferred landscapes is correspondingly more complicated, requiring the application of several of our improvements over the resourceful worm. As closely as I can tell, my own journey of discovery began when I was about four years old, soon after our family moved to a century-old house on two acres of land in the lush, slightly rumpled Pennsylvania countryside south of Lake Erie. It is a region of wooded hills, family farms, and winters that strike like earthquakes. Half the year, it seemed, we spent buried under the rubble, the other half digging out and getting ready for the next shock. The hills are lovely, the farms earnest, well-tended affairs, but it is those winters that give the area its character. Because of them, even in summer a gray pall hangs over the countryside, and a look of endless exhaustion.

During the last century our house served as a landmark for weary travelers plying the dusty road between Erie and Pittsburgh. For a time a large fountain had stood in the front yard. Passersby often stopped there to refresh themselves and their horses. The house became known as the Fountain House. If the fountain had disappeared long before we moved in, the house nevertheless became an important waystation for me, and a wellspring of revelation.

Having lived my entire four years in the nearby city of Meadville, it seemed to me that in emigrating to the country we had removed to a foreign land, and an exotic one at that. The road to the house was still unpaved when we arrived in 1947. Behind the garage there was an out-house, which I remember vividly for its festoons of merry flypaper dangling from the ceiling like party banners. We had walnut trees, wild and very prickly raspberry and blackberry bushes, and six apple trees which produced shiny green apples capable of bringing on a stomachache within thirty seconds. Just beyond the walnut trees I put in a small garden and soon discovered a talent for radishes. Eventually they became my sole crop. My brother raised Angora rabbits, magnificent, enterprising creatures which tended to escape several times a week. A single failing prevented them from making permanent getaways: gluttony. They could always be found not far away in my little garden, munching radishes.

In such a place it was inevitable that I would begin a search, albeit an unconscious one, for a harmonious contour and texture of land. Just beyond our property there was a hill which to my inexperienced eye looked enormous. It was covered with pine trees. One day, probably not long after I moved to the country, several neighborhood children and I entered this vestpocket forest for the first time, and my journey of discovery began. I remember that I was afraid of the place, but at the same time awed by it and drawn to it. Standing at the edge of the wood, peering into the shadows within, I believed I was about to encounter dangers and powers greater than any I had ever faced. Then I took a bold step, probably my first such, and stole in among the crowding trees. I was certain that what I was doing was forbidden.

As the days passed, we children began playing regularly in what we now called "the pines." I continued to be afraid of this dimly lit woodland, but my fear was a quite acceptable variety. It sprang, surprisingly, not from trepidations over unseen evils but from those feelings of wonder and awe that had drawn me into the pines to begin with.

That fear was only one of the place's attractions. The pines felt wholly different from the rest of the world. No matter how warm or bright or bustling the day beyond, inside it was always cool and dark and hushed. The air was permeated with a moist odor of decay, which I loved, and underfoot, in the thick carpet of rusty pine needles, I discovered the pleasure of making my mark and establishing a link between myself and these tall, mysterious trees. In the pines I learned direction and connection; I learned to find my way.

Some things could not be explained. Sometimes we came upon trails through the duff that we had not constructed. These we attributed to Indians. The conviction arose that a bear lived in the woods and that it, too, might have carved the routes. To my knowledge none of us ever saw the bear but at our ages, mercifully, reality was only incidentally a product of the senses.

The final mystery was one that did not seem so at the time but, as the years have passed, has by its nature and its longevity grown to be the greatest mystery of all. It is one not of sight or of sound but of resonance, an echo of a seemingly undistinguished moment in time. Why that moment continues to reverberate within me when a billion others do not, why even four decades after it crept past me feather-light in the forest it recalls itself with the urgency of death, I do not know. There is almost nothing to it. Perhaps five years old, I am standing alone, the straight, rough trunk of a pine tree rising to my left. It is dark and silent in the forest and I feel completely at peace. I look toward the brow of the hill. Above, dapples of blue sky drift downward through the treetops.

What incomprehensible force could have seized that prosaic moment and sealed it upon me with such ferocity? Powered not by tornado or flashing comet but by the simple majesty of pines, it created an image of unfading eloquence, one which, I believe, has helped to determine the direction of my life.

In winter, mighty storms swept down from Ontario and buried the country in snow. The bare hillside beside the pines became a sled-riding course famed throughout the neighborhood. Each afternoon, long trains of Flexible Flyers flew down the slope, five or ten sleds in tandem, one practically atop the next. One day some daredevil among us discovered that by climbing higher and beginning his run in the pines, he could achieve a velocity that induced screams in spectators. As those of us who emulated his feat quickly found out, this was not a stunt for the fainthearted. At the halfway point the sledder had to pull off an almost impossible maneuver, a hard left onto the old path at terrible speed. Any miscalculation, any failure of nerve or of will, and sled and rider were doomed. Across the path they sailed, over the icy lip on the far side, and upside-down into the raspberry bushes.

But success . . . Success was the delicious alternative, and its slim likelihood made the risk of failure decidedly worth taking. Success put us on the old run at a blinding rate, sent us rocketing down the slope, slicing the bitter wind, leaping the nasty bump at the bottom, tearing past the apple trees, past the outhouse, past the terrified Angora rabbits, into the backyard of the Fountain House. And finally, crying from laughter, smack dab onto a patch of ground that during the tender summer days to follow would become, briefly, the world's largest radish garden. What a triumph it was, and what a joy, to absorb the power of the pines at the top of the hill and make it all the way home!

We moved to another town when I was seven, and I didn't see the pines again for many years. When I returned I was amazed, and disappointed, to see how small the area was—perhaps an acre of trees in all, on a hillside that rose gently to a height little greater than that of the house. From the backyard of the Fountain House a short distance away the pines were scarcely noticeable.

And yet it was the pines I was most eager to see. However insignificant my miniature forest may have appeared to others, in me it inspired the same feelings of fear and of awe that it always had. Not many years later, I began seeking out other and deeper forests, as if in a fever, first in New England, later throughout the American West; simultaneously I began exploring peaks and passes and have continued to do so ever since. When emptiness fills my chest, a climb into the country of forests and of mountains is a journey of rediscovery and a coming home. Gathered once more into an embrace of circling trees, I plant my feet in the rich undergrowth and search for the dappled sky.